The Difficult Borderline Personality Patient Not So Difficult to Treat

The Difficult Borderline Personality Patient Not So Difficult to Treat

Understanding Their Psychodynamics as a Guide to Successful and Satisfying Therapy

Helen Garshanin Albanese, MD

Clinical Associate Professor of Psychiatry
University of Texas Health Science Center, San Antonio, Texas

Copyright © 2012 by Helen Garshanin Albanese, MD.

Library of Congress Control Number: 2012911561
ISBN: Hardcover   978-1-4771-3383-5
              Softcover   978-1-4771-3382-8
              Ebook   978-1-4771-3384-2

All rights reserved. No part of this book may be reproduced or transmitted in any form or by any means, electronic or mechanical, including photocopying, recording, or by any information storage and retrieval system, without permission in writing from the copyright owner.

This book was printed in the United States of America.

To order additional copies of this book, contact:
Xlibris Corporation
1-888-795-4274
www.Xlibris.com
Orders@Xlibris.com
87838

Contents

Introduction 9
Chapter 1: Psychodynamics 13
Chapter 2: Therapy..28
Chapter 3: Course of Therapy 39
    Stage I 39
    Stage II...45
        1. The Awareness of the Merger 46
        2. Awareness of How the Merger Is Set Up 47
        3. Connection between Life Events and the Crisis Is Incomplete and Lags in Time 48
        4. Appearance of Guilt and Sorrow..........................49
        5. Exaggerated Sense of Guilt 50
        6. Developing the Ability to Remember Crises and Resolutions over Time.......................................52
    Stage III 53
Chapter 4: Inpatient Treatment 57
Chapter 5: Extended Interpersonal Systems 64
    Approach to the Therapeutic Systems...............................67
        Family Therapy 69
        Group Therapy 76
Chapter 6: Medication 78
Summary and Conclusions 83
Bibliography 87

Dedication

*With gratitude to Dr. David Fuller, who listened, suggested, and encouraged
and who was generous with time, patience, and optimism
and
To all the patients who shared their hearts with me
and
To my family for being there
Thank you!*

Introduction

I have written this book to share with those who are working with borderline personality disorder (BPD) patients a therapeutic approach that I have found helpful in achieving a successful outcome. This therapeutic approach is based on an understanding of the dynamics that underline the BPD person's emotional experience and behavior. It allows for the therapist's individual creativity in dealing with such patients, and it does not involve rote learning of interventions. I wish to clarify that when I talk about BPD patients, I do not mean those who just fit the *Diagnostic and Statistical Manual of Mental Disorders (fourth edition, text revision) (DSM-IV-TR)* diagnostic criteria, but those who, in addition to that criteria, seem to get worse with our usual interventions, yet come back for more.

The goal of this book is not to present a comprehensive review of the literature or examination of all the contributions to the understanding of BPD. I shall not be able to give credit to the many authors who have laid the basis for my understanding and therapeutic approach to BPD patients. The aim of this book is to present how a clear, psychodynamic understanding can be used to conduct therapy with BPD patients effectively. The psychodynamics are drawn from clear evidence of these patients' verbalizations and their interpersonal responses; examples of real patients and real therapeutic interventions are used in this book. My way of dealing with these patients is only one way of doing so. I have seen and heard of what seem to be totally different approaches also having good results. I suggest that all successful approaches with these patients work because they do, in essence, accomplish the same goals dictated by the patient's very own psychodynamics.

Over the many years that I have taught and supervised residents in psychiatry, I have noted that it is the BPD patients who give the greatest difficulties to the residents. This is no surprise since even experienced therapists find it difficult to treat BPD patients. These patients are often thought of with dread and avoidance. I have further noted that the residents feel that the helpful therapeutic approaches already developed, such as the dialectical behavioral therapy, need much training to master. Thus, there remains a prevailing pessimism about therapy with BPD patients. It is that pessimism and sense of difficulty in learning to treat BPD patients that I hope to dispel.

Despite the sense of responsibility and a tremendous wish to help these patients, there is no doubt that fear, insecurity, and pessimism about the therapy is evoked in any empathic therapist. Therefore, often the therapist does not wish to deal with these patients. It is exactly these ambivalent feelings in the therapist that can, paradoxically as it may seem, ultimately lead to improvement in the patient. Understanding the source of these feelings and their function for the patient can lead to a more confident, hopeful, and effective therapy with BPD patients.

As therapists, we learn that a certain repertoire of interventions and interactions will help someone who is suicidal, depressed, psychotic, etc. However, if these problems are found in the patient with BPD, the usual interventions and interactions do not work or may even backfire. Most therapists can learn to accommodate to the unique demands that therapy with the BPD patient requires. It does take time and effort to stop and reinterpret one's emotional responses and actions with these patients. If the therapist is overwhelmed with work, their own personal struggles, or their own narcissistic vulnerability at the moment, or if there are too many patients with similar difficulties as BPD, it is probably wise that the therapist does not attempt to work with BPD patients. Additionally, some therapists are so good in picking up a patient's feelings—too good, in fact—that the emotional work the patient requires is too overwhelming. These therapists can also avoid such patients, knowing they do so not because they are indifferent but because they are too in tune with these patients.

Thus, it is not the unemphatic therapist who does not wish to work with these patients. It is rather the therapist who feels too much for them and who finds it too difficult to be with them who avoids them. It is as if "too much empathy" leads to avoidance of these patients. Actually, these patients do not just make *us* feel for *them*. They evoke in us the same feelings that they have. When we have empathy for someone, we know how that person feels, and we know it is that person who feels that emotion. There is, nonetheless, a recognition that we are separate beings. We are only "putting ourselves in their place"; we may even recall that we have felt the same when in a similar situation. We can say that "we feel happy, sad, angry, etc. *for* them." With the

BPD patient, however, we are not aware that the feelings *we* have are the feelings *the patient* has. We "become" the patient in the feeling realm. We may act on these feelings, unaware that we are patient driven. Most of the time, we struggle with these feelings using our own repertoire of mechanisms of defense. Thus, there is a qualitative difference in the empathy we may feel for another person and the empathy we may feel with the BPD patient. Becoming aware of this quality of the feelings we have for these patients is the first step in putting our relating with these patients in perspective.

I think there are four important elements to keep in mind when dealing with these patients. They are as follows:

1. Understanding the psychodynamics
2. Understanding the feelings we have with these patients
3. Not reacting reflexively with them
4. Taking a therapeutic style that is neither too passive nor too active

BPD patients who fit the *DSM-IV-TR* criteria for diagnosis and who seem to get worse with the usual interventions, invariably also evoke the above-mentioned strong emotional reactions in therapists. These people are arrested at a certain relating level that makes them difficult to deal with. Some of these patients may have been abused in childhood (although it is extremely important to realize that not all were abused). In this book, I shall show how I use a psychodynamic understanding of these patients to create this therapeutic approach. I further hope that the understanding of these patients will give freedom to the readers to create their own therapeutic approaches that they are most comfortable with. Most of all, I hope to make it very clear that the negative feelings these patients evoke are actually in the service of their betterment and thus to instill a sense of control and hopefulness in the therapists. What counts most of all is not what we feel when we first engage with these patients but how we end up feeling with them.

Chapter 1

Psychodynamics

It is worth understanding the psychodynamics of patients with BPD because it explains what they feel and why they feel and act as they do. It also helps to predict their reaction to our interventions. As long as we keep in mind the basic dynamic principles they operate under, we can be flexible and create our own therapeutic interventions with them. Persons with BPD appear to have a problem in experiencing their own self and others as integrated beings, who are sometimes good and sometimes bad. They often perceive themselves and others as overwhelmingly good or bad. The affect that they experience with these states is very intense and can change from one extreme to the other quite rapidly. It follows, therefore, that their interpersonal relationships are extremely tumultuous.

Analysts, such as Mahler (1968), Kernberg (1975), and Masterson (1976), while trying to clarify these phenomena and put it into words, have pointed out that the BPD person is stuck in the separation-individuation phase of development, specifically in the rapprochement subphase of that period.

It is prudent to briefly review what this actually means in the normal intrapsychic development.

The first stage, the earliest child's experience of self and others, is rather undifferentiated. The child feels "as one" with the mother, who satisfies the child's needs for nutrition, physical comfort, and security (maybe as one with anyone who performs the mothering tasks). This interaction is felt as good and soothing. Thus, a me-mom-all-good feeling perception is developed. Soon after, me-mom-all-bad feelings are also developed when pain and discomfort are perceived and experienced in the mother's presence.

Thus, in the second stage of development, two sets of opposite "Self-Mom-Affects" are fixed in the memory of the child. These perceptions are normally kept separate so that when one is experienced, it is as if the other is "not there." The affect accompanying each perception is intense. The separation of these two affects, the "splitting," seems to have a protective function as it assures preservation of the "Me-Mom-All-Good" perception needed for the security of the child.

The third stage of development evolves when the child develops a sense of feeling good and different from the mother. With this sense of being a separate being from the mother, needing, missing, envying, and being afraid of losing the good mother can be experienced. Soon the feeling of the self as bad and in pain, and the feeling that the mother as bad and hurtful are also experienced as separate. Now the child seems to have two opposite and separate affect-experiences of the self and two opposite and separate affect-experiences of the mother; there are now four separate people's experiences. This is the stage of separation-individuation.

The last and fourth stage of development comes with the integration of the good-me and bad-me states and the integration of the good-mom and bad-mom perceptions. The affect is now more subdued during both pleasurable and unpleasurable experiences. The intense rage that was previously experienced at the mother during the "mother as bad and hurtful" affect-experience is now subdued since the affect state of her also being good is there to diminish it. With this, guilt for being "mean" to the good mother arises as the child is able to feel love and hate at the same time. Forgiveness and sorrow can be experienced. At this point, it can be said that the person has a stable self-concept and is whole-object relating.

With BPD, it is observed that the patient behaves as if stuck in the third stage of development, with the intense affect of love or destructiveness toward others who are seen as extremely good or extremely bad.

However, there is a second element that complicates the picture of the BPD patients that is discussed in this book. When the child reaches the separation-individuation stage and feels and perceives the good self as separate from the good mother, the child cannot sustain this separateness from the moment it occurs for the first time. This sense of separateness is accompanied with a sense of weakness and fear as well as a sense of self-exhilaration and strength. The child needs to remerge with the mother and obtain replenishment from her before the next individuation excursion. The process is intrapsychic—it is inside the child's "head and heart." This process is formed by the responses the child receives from the mother alongside the child's experiences of the affect due to its own biological makeup.

Margaret Mahler (1968) identified this in-and-out-of merger with the mother as the rapprochement subphase of the separation-individuation stage. These separations and remergers are very important for the child to be able to finally sustain a stable sense of a separate self.

Mahler (1968) and Masterson (1976) also found that the mother and child, who eventually have BPD, will set up a unique and uninterrupted interaction. The mother is not available for this replenishment and remerger when the child comes to her after exploring and joyfully making its own choices and feeling its own strength. The mother is not in tune with the child and, in reality or emotionally, is experienced by the child as cold and withdrawing. The child is, in effect, abandoned by the mother at the moment the child has just had a joyful experience of self. If the child regresses (throws temper tantrums, is in pain, etc.), then the mother picks up the child and becomes emotionally present; the "two" will become "one" for the moment. This temporary remerger with the mother during the rapprochement subphase of the separation-individuation stage occurs only when the child is regressed and in pain. The child gives up its own individuation and strengths in order to "have its mother." The normal fear of being separate is reinforced by the rejection or abandonment, and the child experiences overwhelming separation panic. This abandonment is dealt with by merger, through pain, to the child. The pain and loss of individuation now serves as the purpose of avoiding the sense of abandonment. The fear of abandonment when feeling individuated and strong, and the rage of being engulfed and stifled (i.e., feeling forced into this situation) go on. The child cannot complete separation-individuation nor integration. The relating with the mother is "perverse."

The rage that is evoked in the child is too great to allow the good-self and the bad-self to integrate. The child feels much less love ("good") than evilness ("bad") toward the mother for the two affects to be experienced at the same time. Because of this great affect intensity, splitting of the self as all-good and all-evil cannot be mended. If there is an attempt to be emotionally in touch with the sense of being evil, at the same time as being good, the feeling of being evil totally overtakes and makes the feeling of being good disintegrate. The defensive function of splitting is now strengthened to preserve the sense of being good. Likewise, the perception of mother who stifles and demands pain, together with projections of the child's own hatred onto the mother, makes the sense of mother being evil too great. This evil mother cannot be mediated by perception and feelings of when she is good to the child. Thus, the splitting also has great value in preserving the existence of the good mother for the child by keeping the perceptions of the bad mother separate. The splitting of the disparate feeling-images of the mother as well as the disparate feeling-perceptions of the self is strengthened. The separation-individuation cannot be maintained, for it leads to abandonment, and the remerger cannot be maintained, for it impinges on awareness of pleasantness of selfhood. The child continues to struggle for separation-individuation with a vulnerability to feeling abandonment, especially when doing well, and a sense of painful engulfment (as a consequence of the remerger) when doing poorly. Indeed, there is no good way to go for this person.

While many patients may fit the *DSM-IV-TR* criteria for BPD and may show affective intensity, instability, fear of abandonment, and may even use similar defense mechanisms, I shall be talking only about those who, in addition, show what I have termed "perverse relating." A hallmark of this perverse relating is that when patients approach a therapist with various serious complaints, they will react to any help the therapist provides with a message of "that is not good enough and is hurting me." They react to the help as engulfing, crushing, and annihilating as being forced to submerge themselves to the therapist's will. In contrast to someone with narcissistic personality disorder (NPD), who may also give us the message "that is not good enough," the BPD patient will then pursue the therapist with increased complaints, asking for more help. The NPD patient will, however, "throw us away" at this point and will not come with further demands for help or will somehow decide that they were the ones who came up with the help the therapist provided, and thus they are "better." The BPD patient's insistence that the therapist helps them, followed by their deterioration, creates in the therapist a sense of frustration, fear, and a desire to avoid the patient. The therapist feels there is no good way to go; they feel cornered.

This is seen when the patient comes to the emergency room because of severe suicidal ideation, having perhaps taken pills or cut themselves, and then refusing to be admitted, forcing the therapist to insist and, at times, commit the patient. Another characteristic situation is when therapists have been forced to give an ever-increasing number of various medications in increasing doses with minimal relief to the patient and abounding side effects. At times, even our diagnoses may change from depression to depression-with-psychosis, bipolar disorder, schizophrenia, substance-abuse disorder, panic disorder, eating disorder, and so on. The less experience a therapist has with this type of patient, the more anxious, afraid, frustrated, and enraged the therapist becomes. Any efforts to help can result in a constant increase in the number of sessions and even focusing much more on the patient than the therapist normally would on other patients. At times, therapists have gone to patients' homes, acted as their chauffer, talked to them at any hour of the day or night—all in effort to stop some (seemingly imminent) catastrophe for the patient, such as suicide or violence. The therapists, by definition, feel they must help the patient and prevent such catastrophes. Meanwhile, the patient's intense emotions and threatening behavior will escalate. This can become, quite simply, a nightmare.

Case 1.1

A patient was admitted to the state hospital because of attempted suicide by an overdose of medication. All usual and appropriate treatment was instituted—medication, one-to-one observation, and even electric shock therapy. One year later, the patient was still unable to be discharged because his suicidal behavior had progressed to cutting his throat superficially multiple times. He had to be monitored even when using the bathroom. This patient was not psychotic and had no history of substance abuse or any organic brain syndrome.

Case 1.2

A patient was in outpatient therapy with a very good-hearted, empathic, young psychiatry resident. The patient increased his suicidal ideation and started mentioning the gun he had. When told to get rid of it, instead, he actually brought the gun out for the therapist to hold. Out of fear, the therapist held the gun. In a few weeks, the patient came to his session with another loaded gun, pointed it at himself, and said he would shoot himself. At this point, the therapist wanted to get up and seek help as they were in a room without a phone. The patient responded by explaining that if the therapist left the room, he would definitely shoot himself. The therapist was a hostage for four hours before he finally left to ask for help. The patient did not shoot himself.

Another side of these cases is that as the patients demonstrate their pain and frightening symptoms, provoking the therapist into helping activities, they also complain that the therapist has been unfair to them, as if the therapist has invaded their freedom and individuality.

Case 2.1

A patient admitted to the hospital for suicidal behavior sat in a small group of patients and staff. He talked of his suicidal wishes. As all group members attempted to talk him out of suicide, he only became more adamant that he would have to kill himself. In exasperation, the group members gave up and changed the subject. As everyone was getting up at the end of the session, he said, "I want at least one of you to give me one good reason why I should not kill myself." At this point, the therapists could not allow the members of the group to leave with this burden of responsibility that the patient had placed on them. One of the therapists said that since the patient was in the hospital, he would be watched, helped, would not be allowed to hurt himself, and would not be discharged until he was better. To that, the patient said, "How dare you tell me I cannot kill myself! It is my life!" Note here the switch from "Help me—stop me from killing myself" to "You are intruding on me too much."

The patient in this case is demonstrating a need or someone to take over as he is in despair and unable to do it for himself. As he does receive the help he has requested, he then switches to experiencing this help as an unpleasant stifling, in other words, a merger.

Case 2.2

A female patient said that she had told her husband that life was not worth it and that suicide was the answer. Since she had a history of suicidal attempts in the past, the husband took her medicine from her so she would not hurt herself. She recounted that this act of his made her feel very stifled and complained that the husband gives her no freedom.

It is of note that she did not say that she would kill herself after that intervention by the husband. His help temporarily relived her of the suicidal feelings and immediately made her feel too stifled. The help was felt as an unpleasant merger.

Case 2.3

A woman, who frequently, on and off, is either suicidal or "unable" to do anything around the house or even drive, complained that the husband—who thus took charge of her medicine, did the housework, and drove her—was making her feel stifled.

Before he had to leave town for a week for his work, she became very distraught and "depressed" with hints of suicide, which she made clear to the husband. After he left, she became energetic and did many things around the house and in the garden. However, she did have daily conversations with the husband who continued to express his concern for her, which she said bothered her. She said, "Why is he treating me like that?"

His concern not only relived her of suicidal feeling but also again made her feel stifled. She also demonstrated that she was unable to connect her behavior (being suicidal) to the husband's responses.

Case 2.4

A young woman, who is supported in college by her parents, described being totally unable to pay her bills on time, to maintain a budget, or to keep track of money in her checking account. In almost the same sentence, she complained that her parents give her no freedom or respect as an adult by setting up automatic bill payments and doling out money to her.

Through such examples, we get a glimpse that help, though sought out by such patients, is experienced by them as an unpleasant merger. Yet they continue to ask for this help-merger and at the same time long to feel more individuated, well, and strong. It is important to realize that this merger is both sought and repelled by the patient. The patient seeks the merger whenever threatened by abandonment and can be observed to be in extreme emotional crisis during the abandonment experience. Any observer of this situation is totally convinced of the seriousness of the patient's plight and feels the patient's distress. This is in contrast to the emotional remonstrations of a patient with histrionic personality disorder, whose pain does not touch the therapist as deeply. With the BPD patient, the perception of abandonment is followed in quick succession by the patient feeling intolerable separation fear, followed by self-infliction of emotional and physical pain and regression. This self-inflicted pain always involves a witness, whether in reality or fantasy, with a resulting relief of the abandonment feeling. However, now arise the discomfort and rage at being in the situation of pain and loss of individuality.

By recognizing the painful self-inflictions and loss of function of these patients as a means of achieving mergers, an explanation arises for the unusual shifting of the various modes of self-hurting behavior and contradictory abilities in function these patients can show.

Case 3.1

A middle-aged woman explained in detail how she was thinking of hurting herself during the time in which she functioned very well as a babysitter for her daughter, who was working full-time. The patient also recounted that during the same time she was making detailed plans to open a business for herself and had taken concrete steps to do so. However, though extremely responsible in child care, she has no idea what medication she takes. Her husband has been doling out her medication to her for years. When in the depressed and suicidal state, which she says hits her suddenly, she feels unable to get out of bed, do anything, and is preoccupied with images of suicide. Usually, her husband tries to help her, makes her get out of bed, go out to eat with him, and so on. She always rejects and fights his suggestions while making it clear that she is in bad shape. When, at one time, he did not force her to get out of bed, she said to him, "I could always count on you in the past. Now I cannot even do that." She later explained to me, "He should know I cannot make decisions when I am depressed." On the same day as this incident, she later got up on her own, cared for her grandchild, and made a decision to take the sick child to the doctor.

The loss of ability to function was in a specific area: functions that, when he was around, her husband would usually take over during her "depressed" state. One part of her regressed, while another part of her was highly functional. The "inability" she experienced and showed was in relation to the mergers with her husband.

Case 3.2

A patient, who had been hospitalized for suicidal behavior, became very agitated and verbally assaultive, gesticulating threateningly. The attendants came to restrain her and a struggle ensued, with the patient held down on the floor. Later, the patient said, "The moment they put their hands on me, I thought 'It is up to them to control me now.'"

The patient's loss of control increased in response to the availability of reciprocating control.

Case 3.3

A patient, while in front of all in a hospital day room, was seriously hurting herself with insulin overdoses and attempted to hang herself. When it became necessary to transfer her to an open unit because of the need for beds for sicker patients, she said, "They have open doors in that unit. I guess I will have to control myself there."

These examples demonstrate that the function which is lost depends on the reciprocal response(s) of those around the patient. Indeed, it can be repeatedly observed that the patient almost always functions better out of the hospital setting, better than the staff could ever imagine. It can even seem that if there was nobody to respond to the patient, the patient could do well.

However, it is not true that the patient could sustain a sense of well-being or consistent functioning if there was nobody around to respond to their bids for merger, and this is because of two reasons:

The first reason is the normal need for remerger in the developing individual. The exhilaration of individuation and strength is also frightening initially, and there is a need to return to the safety of a temporary remerger with the mother. The BPD person has not completed the individuation process—they have not consolidated the sense of a strong, individuated self. The patient, therefore, needs these temporary remergers to complete the separation-individuation work. Unfortunately, the patient will set up the remergers to be as they have always experienced them with an eventual outcome that causes pain to themselves.

The second reason they need the remerger is more specific to the patient with BPD. For them, the sense of individuation and strength is also associated with feelings of abandonment, which makes the need for remerger imperative. They inevitably fail at the endeavor of good functioning and the sense of well-being as, to them, it means abandonment. Through some crisis, they recapture the sense of merger, thus avoiding individuation and the concomitant feeling of abandonment. The form of the crisis can change depending on the reciprocal response of those around, but the crisis is necessary for their emotional survival through their horrendous separation anxiety.

At times the patients, without direct statements on their part, will show us their pain so that we are forced to conclude that they are in a desperate state.

Case 4.1

A patient went to her family practitioner and said, "I am going to get off my antidepressant, and I want you to help me do it."

The physician responded with "oh! you must be feeling so good! I am glad!"

"No," the patient replied, "actually I am feeling worse than ever."

Of course, the doctor then said, "No, I am not going to help you get off your medication." According to the patient, the doctor left the room at this point.

As the patient reported this incident, she said, "I threw this bomb, and the doctor did not even ask why I was saying those things. She did not care if I died or not."

It seems rather likely, however, that the doctor did pick up the patient's message that she wanted to hurt herself, and that she was inviting the doctor to collaborate in this self-hurt. The doctor probably left feeling shocked, impotent, angry, and maybe glad that the patient had a psychiatrist to deal with such things.

The communication of wanting to hurt herself was indirect.

Case 4.2

One morning, a patient's husband casually asked what she would do that day. The patient said to her husband, "Oh! I have my plans. You just go on to work." Since she had been suicidal multiple times in the past, he became concerned at the tone of her voice and the word "plans" and stayed home that day. She later told me that she was aware that the word "plans" would concern him.

Case 4.3

A patient called his psychiatrist on the phone and said, "I have saved all my pills and did not take them, but I will not come to see you or get any treatment again." This patient had taken overdoses several times in the past. Again the doctor picked up the obvious message *I will hurt myself*, although it was not explicitly verbalized.

Sometimes the patient sits in front of a therapist without speaking, with such a look on their face that the therapist can become very concerned. The patient will answer very few questions, or does so only in short syllables, and will be evasive in their responses to questions about self-hurt. The therapist can become so concerned that they find themselves speaking for the patient. A few minutes later, this same patient might be observed with friends, speaking fluently and with animation.

All these cases are examples of how the patient can seduce us and induce us to be more sensitive and perceptive about them with our emotional "antennas." They induce us to feel with them, think for them, and do for them. We feel "sucked" into them—a definite merger.

It is of interest that the therapist's emotional responses often mirror the patient's emotional state. The fear and terror the therapist feels (while contemplating doing nothing—abandoning the patient—is unthinkable) that something catastrophic will happen mirrors the patient's terror about abandonment. The therapist's sense of an imperative need to solve the situation mirrors the patient's urgent need to get out of the insupportable emotional state. Both the therapist and the patient also share the utter sense of impotence, helplessness, frustration, and feelings of being "bad" people. Finally, the therapist feels entrapped as all efforts fail, without relief from the painful and overwhelming affective tie to the patient. The therapist may feel rage and a wish to get rid of the patient. Fantasies may occur of chastising the patient, such as saying "then just kill yourself!" or "I don't care!" There is a sense of a desire to violently throw the patient away. Sometimes the therapist actually arranges to transfer the patient to another therapist. This desire to get rid of the patient mirrors the patient's own desire to get rid of the painful and regressive merger with the therapist. It is what the patient experiences when they say, "how dare you tell me I cannot kill myself!", or "they give me no freedom," or "he is stifling me!" and so forth.

The mirroring of the patient's affect is also a clue as to what is going on between the patient and the therapist, or anyone the patient has engaged in an emotional situation. As discussed above, a merger occurs that is felt by both the patient and the therapist. This is an affective merger. It is definitely initiated by the patient and always in the setting of a crisis. However, once the therapist has entered into the emotional merger, both the patient and the therapist have a role in how the emotional crisis will end at the moment. If the therapist becomes totally lost in the fear, urgency, and helplessness, the patient will continue to reverberate with this and may act out on the overwhelming affect. If the therapist does not enter into the emotional merger (i.e., they are totally unperturbed), the patient will continue to be overwhelmed by the affect and will again either act on the feeling and possibly hurt themselves or seek someone else who will enter into the emotional merger. The healing of the abandonment and extreme separation anxiety is imperative, and the merger is indispensable.

The experience of this seemingly hopeless situation can evoke a nihilistic attitude in many therapists, forcing them to shun the BPD patient.

Observation of these patients over a long period of time, however, can show that while some do commit suicide, the majority do not do so even though they have a great number of suicide attempts. The patients will also always have episodes (short in duration at first) of doing remarkably well. As they get older, they become less and less emotionally overwhelming. First, the therapist and then, much later, the patient will come to see that totally helpless situations are episodic and transient—in the long run; the situation is *not* hopeless.

A clue as to what is most helpful to these patients can be found by observing the outcomes of each emotional merger they get into. Although the outcome can be an escalation of the hurtful behavior by the patient, there is at least a temporary quenching of the emotional turbulence. This calming occurs especially when the emotional-merger partner ends up regaining a semblance of equanimity during the emotional crisis. Ogden (1982) has identified this process that goes on between the patient and the therapist as projective identification. It is the process in which the patient induces the therapist to feel the same affect as the patient feels. When they are in the same affective state, the patient follows emotionally how the therapist handles the affect. In essence, an emotional resonance is set up between the two, where the affect is initiated and given the quality and initial intensity by the patient. The handling and the eventual intensity of the affect, however, are in the hands of the therapist. I find that a more descriptive name for this "projective identification" is "patient-induced emotional resonance." I shall use this term whenever I refer to the projective-identification process.

When an emotional resonance is set up, the following three elements are involved:

1. The patient will feel an overwhelming affect, with the need for immediate relief.
2. The patient will induce the same affect in another person, which is inescapable. While this inducement may be conscious, most of the time it is unconscious.
3. The patient will copy how the person (in whom the affect has been induced) handles this affect.

This situation involves an emotional merger of the two people involved and serves to help the initiator to handle the overwhelming affect. The emotional resonance then serves to provide both a relief of abandonment via merger and a way of handling the overwhelming concomitant affect. When the patient feels abandoned by a person, the affect is overwhelming and the abandoning person is felt as extremely evil. This affect is handled either by emotional resonance or has to be acted out. The self-hurting behavior, hints, and threats mainly aim to accomplish the setup of the emotional resonance and, therefore, temporary healing of the overwhelming affects accompanying the perceived abandonment, by abolishing the sense of separateness.

The aim is not to die but to be helped via the merger experience.

Case 5.1

After a suicidal episode, a patient said, "I am afraid I may really kill myself if there is no one around. I don't mean I need someone to stop me from killing myself—I mean if there is no one there to listen to me." She expressed her understanding that she was seeking something else than being directly stopped from suicide; she was seeking someone to listen to her. If that was not available, she was afraid she might actually kill herself. She made it clear that she did not need someone to talk her out of suicide, but rather she needed "someone to listen." As this other person(s) listened to the patient, the emotional resonance was set up and provided relief.

It is the essence of that interaction that she found lifesaving. She was also aware that she did not want to die.

Case 5.2

Another patient made this clear when I was called to do a consultation interview of a patient for an inpatient staff conference. The patient had a clear history and findings of BPD. I had thirty minutes to interview and interacted with him, and I mainly paid attention to the emotional resonance setup with the two of us. I sweated a lot. What I said to him at that time was, "Mr. A, I see that you have had a very hard time and have suffered a lot for a long time. It seems many things have been tried to help you. Nothing really worked well. You even have many side effects with little or no benefit from the medication. The staff on this unit do not know what else to do and have called me to see if I can suggest something. As we have talked, I have been thinking very hard about what I can do to help, for I very much want to help and can feel your pain . . . (pause) . . . I cannot think of anything new to suggest. I don't know . . . (pause) . . . I feel your fear and am very frustrated and feel bad that I cannot take the pain away . . . (pause) . . . I feel frustrated and bad, the way you must feel . . . (pause) . . . Right now, maybe all I can do is sit here with you, feeling bad together." This patient continued to talk of suicide and emotionally involve me, and I continued to say a variation of the above for most of the thirty minutes. After the patient left the room and the staff and I talked for another thirty minutes, I left the meeting room.

As I walked down the corridor, the patient met me and said, "Dr. Albanese, I want to talk to you again. It helped so much." Why? Did I give any suggestions to help him? No. I was overtly the most unhelpful and ignorant doctor he probably ever met. Yet he felt that I helped him. The staff confirmed that he was better for a while after the interview. Evidently, I had helped him digest and subdue the overwhelming affect as it was shared in the emotional resonance between us. I definitely did feel afraid, frustrated, and bad, but I was not lost in the affect and I tolerated it. The patient resonated with this and calmed down. He experienced help with his overwhelming affect.

I said that the above patient experienced temporary relief and was no longer suicidal. It must be noted that this is temporary. It is important to realize that if he was praised subsequently for improving much and for "doing so well" on the unit (as he was), he would revert, seemingly inexplicably, to being extremely depressed, and a cycle of patient-staff desperation would start again. I say "inexplicably" because there would be no evident rejection, criticism, or any bad event.

There is often no obvious abandonment to which the BPD patient is so vulnerable. But actually doing well and, in particular, being praised for doing well can trigger the BPD person to feel abandonment. This can be observed repeatedly and can baffle the therapist. After a session when the patient did well and the therapist encouraged the patient with praise and "boosting the self-esteem" in the next session, the patient might be in a desperate situation again. This is less baffling if we remember that the patient is stuck in the separation-individuation phase. He can tolerate being separate for only a short time (just as any emotional toddler) and needs reassurance of a remerger for the moment. In the case of the BPD patient, he also predicts that he cannot get this sustenance of the remerger when he is doing well. He expects disconnection and rejection after doing well. He reads praise as rejection and abandonment—a refusal on the therapist's part for the required temporary remerger. This automatically increases his fear and doubles his effort for a remerger via his only known means—threatening or doing self-harm, with concomitant fear and rage.

This negative reaction to praise can be immediate or delayed, and it differentiates the patient with BPD from the patient with NPD. The BPD patient is threatened by praise, and the NPD patient blooms with it.

As I have discussed different dynamic points above, it can be noted that the patient's emotional turbulence occurs mainly when the patient perceives abandonment or feels threatened by the possibility of abandonment. This can occur when the patient is losing a relationship (including losing a doctor, teacher, or therapist) permanently or temporarily, such as during vacation times. Also any negative emotion directed toward the BPD patient, such as anger, is experienced by them as abandonment. Withdrawal of the usual material support, advice, or decision-making is experienced as emotional abandonment more than as a physical threat. Abandonment is also felt when the previously engaging partner in the emotional resonance is refusing to participate any longer. The partner may give the message as this: "I don't care anymore. You always threaten," or "You are always in a crisis. I cannot be upset any longer." However, as noted above, doing well and being happy can also trigger the fear of abandonment. The patient is constantly at the incipient individuation stage when remerger (rapprochement) is needed. While the exhilaration of individuation normally brings the threat of the possibility of abandonment to anyone having to master the separation-individuation phase, it is doubly threatening to a person who has had myriad previous experiences where individuation and feeling strong were actually followed by disconnection, rejection, and abandonment.

Thus, the BPD person does not need an outward threat of abandonment to become a victim of abandonment fears. Their own internal susceptibility to the fear of abandonment and their automatic expectation of abandonment can trigger overwhelming affects and, ultimately, they use self-hurting behavior to seek mergers.

Chapter 2

Therapy

As with patients in general, when working with the BPD patient, therapists are faced with the following questions: "What do we hope to accomplish? What are the treatment goals?" Since the BPD patient usually comes to the therapist in crisis, the immediate goal is to help the patient diminish the affective state and dangerous behavior. In other words, the therapist has to deal with the crisis. The crisis is usually suicidal but may be any of the myriad of ways that such people can hurt themselves or frighten others. It can happen that all of the therapist's efforts are toward this goal of crisis intervention, again and again, with pauses of peace for the patient and the therapist, during which the patient may not even come to therapy. The therapist can become so relieved with the lull in the storm that their mind becomes resistant to any other therapeutic goal for fear that the therapist will bring on more trouble.

I have found that early identification of BPD in the patient and early long-term goal-setting is actually most helpful in dealing with the crises in the short run and in providing a sense of security to the therapist and the patient in the long run. It is helpful that the whole process in its entirety is seen with the immediate emotional turbulence being only a step on the long road to being much better.

Looking at the dynamics of BPD patients in general, it can be seen that certain predictions can be made. Therefore, the long-range goals have to include the following three objectives:

1. Reversal of the perverse relating that the patient has set up has to be accomplished before further growth can occur.

Feeling merged with others when in pain and feeling abandoned when well has to change to feeling received in a merger when well and diminishing the sense of merger when in pain. This change can be noticed when the patient is able to share the "feeling well" feeling with the therapist and continues to come to therapy.

The patient should be able to accept the therapist's praise and sharing of joy with them, without leaving the session suddenly in turmoil again or returning in a crisis. At the same time, the patient should be able to accept the therapist's direct support and encouragement when feeling bad without feeling stifled and without being angry at the therapist and escalating the turmoil.

This reversal of the perverse relating takes a long time, even years. It is most crucial, however, for the patient's well-being. It can be predicted that this benign relating will come in periods that become progressively longer in duration and are interrupted by periods of regression to the original perverse relating when the patient is very threatened by abandonment.

2. Mending the splitting is also a long-term goal.

However, only when the reversal of the perverse relating is accomplished can the patient pick up the unfinished business of individuation: separation and subsequent integration of the split perceptions of self and others. The patient's extreme perceptions of the therapist and others as all-good or as all-bad—without emotionally being able to recall the opposite at any one time (splitting)—can be mended only when the affects, particularly the negative ones, are not overwhelming. This happens when the affects are not in the context of a needed merger at the expense of the patient's well-being and individuation. When the patient is experiencing the therapist as extremely uncaring, it can help to recall their perception of the therapist in the past as being very good, although often it does go from one ear through the other without much emotional value to the patient. It can be predicted that this type of observation for the patient will seem useless for a long time while the patient is still working on diminishing the affective states tied in with abandonment and is consolidating the individuation via benign relating and not perverse relating. In other words, the patient first has to experience mergers after doing well.

The patients will then often start integrating their own all-good and all-bad perceptions of themselves and the therapists on their own. When this integration occurs, the patient may say "I feel so guilty . . ."

The patient is now aware that they have been very angry at, or "mean" to, the same therapist whom they have also loved and felt was good to themselves (i.e., this indicates the integration of the bad and good self). Alternatively, the patient may say, "How can you stand me . . . I gave you such a hard time . . ." This sorrow for the therapist shows that the patient can perceive the therapist as the one who is good to them as well as the one who was "bad" to them (i.e., sorrow for the therapist indicates integration of the good and bad therapist). Another clue that integration is on the way is that the patient can recall and tell the story of various good and bad experiences with a person at the same retelling. An example of this is for a patient to say "I know my husband cares for me when he shows worry and concern about me. It is nice that he cares, but sometimes it is too much, and I do better when he is not around."

As it can be expected that the benign relating will be episodic and temporary for a long while, it can also be expected that the patient will be able to experience guilt and sorrow only episodically at first.

3. A third long-term goal for the patient is to enable them to handle the overwhelming affects in other ways than by emotional resonance with others. Essentially, this means using other "mechanisms of defense," and employing other means of diminishing and handling overwhelming affects.

   The patient will be using the emotional resonance throughout much of their relating with the therapist in the beginning. It is this emotional resonance that is the most powerful tool for the growth of the patient. It is through this means that the patient diminishes the intensity of the affect. The splitting of the affects does not provide diminishment of affect intensity but only avoidance of opposite affects. It should be remembered that the patient-induced emotional resonance serves to reduce the affect for the patient and to provide a merger for the patient. The goal is that this patient-induced emotional resonance is used in a conscious manner by the therapist for the good of the patient.

   The fact that the patient has picked up other mechanisms of defense is seen when the patient talks of emotionally laden events and thoughts without evoking a tremendous urgency that the feelings must be relieved for the patient by the therapist.

Thinking in the above terms and goals, I shall now describe how I go about the therapy of a patient with BPD.

In the initial period, I gather information as quickly as possible. I look for emotional turbulence, self-hurting behavior, and mixed diagnoses given by other therapists or considered by me. I look for evidence that the patient has engaged in perverse relating as I have described it above. Sometimes the patient will talk of a person who has obviously tried to help the patient. Despite the patient's clear desire for this help, the helping person will be perceived as too controlling and intrusive.

At other times, when the patient is too deeply in a crisis to provide a good history and other sources of their history are unavailable, I proceed to offer direct help as I would to any other patient with similar problems. At the same time, however, I very consciously look out for any escalation of symptoms and the establishment of perverse relating and patient-induced emotional resonance with me. If I see that the patient is getting worse while pursuing me for more help and accuses or hints that I am controlling and hurting with my help, I then switch to the mode I use with BPD patients.

The first specific intervention I use when I suspect a patient has BPD is to be very conscious that I am part of the patient-induced emotional resonance. Now, instead of promising directly or indirectly to help and provide relief to the patient, I put in words the feelings we share. I know what these feelings are, for I am also feeling them. Most of the time it is something like the following:

1. "I see you are suffering so much with ... (whatever the patient told me) ... for so long ... (if patient described a long history)."
2. "I want so much to help you," ... (pause) ... "It seems the medicines (I or others gave, or I specifically mention the interventions anyone tried) do not help." ... (pause) ... "If anything, things are worse."
3. "I feel so bad and frustrated that I cannot do more." ... (pause) ... "I just don't know."
4. "I imagine you feel very bad and frustrated that you are suffering so, and no one helps."
5. "Maybe all we can do now is be here together and feel bad—for now."

This is a direct acceptance of the patient's evoked feelings in me—with no further action on my part except telling the patient about my own feelings. In this process, I am using intellectualization and am digesting the feeling into a more tolerable form for myself and the patient. Thus, I am not overwhelmed with feeling and do not act hysterically or impulsively. I tolerate the affect. It is important to note that I never say to the patient "you have made me feel bad by what you said (or did)." That would be accusing the patient of actions with the intent to hurt me. Though these patients are usually unconscious about how they make people feel, occasionally they know what they are doing and their effect on others. But the purpose of their interactions is not to express anger at us or have sadistic joy. The purpose is to relieve their own similar feelings and to feel united with someone temporarily. The patient always has the same feelings as those that they have induced in us. The patient never totally rids themselves of the feeling by putting it into us as in the case of pure projections. The patient requires a *partner* in handling the overwhelming affect.

If I have been correct in my assumption that the patient is inducing emotional resonance in me, I will observe a relief in the patient subsequent to the above intervention. The patient may say that they feel better or demonstrate it by an obvious indication, such as relief in their face, changing to a more optimistic subject, or in their general emotional tone. This relief can be seen very soon after the interaction or it may take some time with repeated variations of the above. Once I see this relief, I know that patient-induced emotional resonance is occurring between us and that I now have a means by which to help the patient. Now I can feel a bit more secure. It is important to remember, however, that while the patient will temporarily calm down, I, as a therapist (and perhaps as one who cannot split easily), will retain some discomfort about the patient for a while.

At this point, I use all my intellectual ability to put in perspective the patient's situation and especially the patient's crises that will recur. During the lull of the emotional turmoil, as the patient talks about themselves and the people around them and their life experiences, there usually comes a clear story of perverse relating with others, as described in chapter 1. Once I have a very clear and specific story of such perverse relating in their life, I know that I am working with a person with BPD as I have described it in this book. Now I can discuss the therapeutic goal as I see it with the patient. I use specific words and examples that the patient has given to me.

Case 6.1

A woman in her thirties, with multiple suicidal attempts in the past, told her husband that she had been thinking of suicide. When the husband, in response to her statement, took the medications from the medicine cabinet and was doling them out to her, she complained that she felt very controlled and stifled.

I said to her, "As you told me your story, I noticed that you seemed to have had people's love and closeness (here I put my hand at my chest)—your husband's—mostly when you felt bad. It is nice to be cared for when in trouble, but as you said, that also feels stifling, like when your husband is controlling your medicine. It is as if you cannot have closeness when you feel strong and well."

The patient acknowledged this and said, "When I do well, I also feel empty."

Patients usually have some acknowledgment of the truth of the statement, especially if specific events and words of the patient are recalled.

After establishing with the patient the above dilemma, I now concretely specify our task. "Since you do not seem to have had the experience of having someone with you (I put my hand on my chest) when you feel well and strong and had mainly someone, like your husband, with you when in distress, you and I may get into relating the same way. It seems to me that our task is that you learn to be together—that you know you have me (I put my hand on my chest) when you are also feeling well and strong. If not, things could only get worse; I mean, you having to feel worse just to come and be with me. I know that you will not be able to believe that you can have someone (I put my hand on my chest) when you feel strong. It will feel like I am asking you to step over a deep cliff and to believe me that you will not fall off. Yet I think that is our main job—to learn to be together and for you to be well."

At this point, I set up parameters of therapy which are different from what I do with some other patients, such as very depressed patients. With the very depressed patients and most of the other patients, I tell them that they can call me anytime they need me. I do not mind being called in the evenings or on weekends. I may not respond immediately, but I will as soon as I can. With the BPD patient, however, I offer a different arrangement.

Right after, I set up the goal of changing my relating with the patient. I say as follows:

Because of this, it would be better that if you are in crisis, you do not call me but wait for the next session to talk about the crisis. If you feel in danger of hurting yourself, go to the emergency room and when you are out, we shall look at what happened. But if you just wish to have a little contact with me or share some happiness, I do not mind being called at three in the morning. I mean that—three in the morning. I may be a little sleepy, but I'd be glad to hear from you and say 'Hi!' If I were to go with you to the hospital and be there for you (I put my hand on my chest) only when you are in pain, I would be hurting you in the long run.

The above can be said only because of the following reasons:

1. There are specific events related by the patient where help was considered stifling.
2. The patient is able to acknowledge an inner loneliness at times.
3. The patient has had some experience of relief with me via the emotional resonance between us.
4. The patient has been given unlimited availability for contact (i.e., merger) when feeling well: the 3:00-a.m. calls.

It always amazes me how many people will accept this arrangement. This is probably because I say this to them when they are not in crisis (I can also say that, so far, no one has called me at three in the morning!). However, if I only said to the patient "if you hurt yourself (or engage in whatever hurtful behavior they have exhibited), I can no longer work with you," the patient would simply not return, crisis or not.

Note that this goal setting with the patient may take a few sessions as data is gathered and emotional turbulence is dampened. I also do not specifically set the goal of diminishing the suicidal or other self-hurting behavior with the patient. If I did that, I may be inadvertently threatening the patient's only self-soothing behavior, and I may be inviting perverse relating with me.

After the above goals are set and discussed, therapy continues by listening and talking with the patient about whatever she brings up. However, I am attuned to every bid for merger with me via pain for the patient and any rejection of my praise or joy for the patient. A long period of work follows where the following five considerations must be taken into account:

1. I never praise or show joy for the patient for a long time. When I do so inadvertently, I see an expected increase of complaints and crises.

    I interpret this for the patient as follows:

    Last time I was so happy for you when you told me of the good work you were doing. It must have felt good (actually I am not sure it felt good to the patient yet; I am implanting the idea that it is OK to feel good under those circumstances), but it may have frightened you. It might have felt as if I did not understand that underneath you still feel weak and afraid, as if I was abandoning you to your inner weakness. Now you are feeling worse and can experience me with you again.

2. When the patient herself experiences well-being and enthusiasm in one session, it is very likely that she will be feeling horrible again in the next session.

    I again interpret that her feeling strong and good with me in the previous session felt nice but also scary. "Maybe it is scary that I may not know you still need me and I may reject you and not be with you (I put my hand on my chest). Today, you feel worse and can feel me with you."
3. I do not specifically address whatever means the patient uses to hurt herself. I always think of any self-hurting behavior as a means for merger with another person.

Case 7.1

If a patient is overspending, I do not lecture and help setup budgets and so forth. I only try to identify who is entering in the perverse relating with her over the particular hurtful behavior. I talk with the patient about her need for union (maybe with her parents, friends, partner, me, etc.). I point out the discrepancy between the patient's abilities in other areas (school, children, etc.) and her inability to manage her own budget. I comment that she certainly has the ability to do so but does not use this ability, for the need to feel closeness to the person who does it for her is greater. I also point out that to achieve this closeness, she is willing to lose money and lose control of her money. Her need to feel with someone (I touch my chest) is so great.

The patient usually denies feeling good with such relating and complains of not having control of her own money. I totally agree then with the patient that the arrangement must feel stifling as similar situations felt in the past when someone took over for her (I recall the examples she has previously described). Then I ask if there are some nice things she can do together with the "stifling" person. Most of the time the relating to this person has become limited to the perverse interactions with the patient being in crisis, or pain, or "messing up," and the other person helping to no avail, resulting in both parties feeling frustrated and unable to stop. I ask the patient to think hard about what she and the other person might do together and both enjoy. I may make suggestions, such as going out to eat, but I insist that the patient chooses something herself. I also warn her that this may seem impossible and empty at first, but it may be worth the try. I make sure to point out that after all the difficulties the two have had neither had given up on the other. This is important, for abandonment is the greatest fear these patients have.

I deal with any other self-hurting behavior or complaint in the same manner.

Case 7.2

A patient talks of having thoughts of cutting herself whenever she sees a knife, of planning what dress she will wear for the funeral, and that her family will be better off without her. She is even sure they would not feel bad if she died. She states she has never felt this bad before, although I have heard this statement and variations of it from her multiple times in the past (in fact, all these patients will behave as if they have never had a similar feeling before). I definitely feel very concerned and worried for her. I feel I must save her, hospitalize her, and get rid of the burden of the responsibility. However, somewhere in the farther recesses of my mind, I do remember that she and I have lived through these feelings multiple times before without any catastrophe occurring and with her switching to totally opposite feelings. I remember that she complained bitterly when her husband tried to protect her in the past by hospitalizing her and that she signed herself out the next day. I also have to force myself to think about abandonment, union via pain, and the sharing of feelings the patient is experiencing. It is hard for me, at the time, to have full confidence in my professional abilities under such a strong, emotional push.

Therefore, I make myself take some time and stay with these feelings without jumping to solutions immediately. I say to her, "You are feeling so bad, so desperate, so helpless, so afraid, so frustrated ... I want to help you ... I don't know ... we are both feeling the same now ... as we did before ... We have to live through this as we did before ... If I send you to the hospital, I remember how much worse you felt then ... I also remember that in the past, you felt very bad ... and then you felt good again ..." When she repeats that she has never felt this bad, I say, "Never this bad ..." but I do not point out that she always says the same thing. I then attempt to inquire as to what happened just before these feelings came. This attempt to correlate the emotional crisis to external events may not be successful. It may seem that the emotional crisis has occurred simply because "the brain malfunctioned." However, I register in my own mind that we must explore whatever has precipitated this crisis at some point in the future.

4. I am also always aware that the patient may set me up to hold her back from growth and autonomy. This is a replay of their past experiences

with parental figures. The patient may tell me of a plan to go to school or take a difficult job in the midst or right after some terrible self-hurting crisis or after demonstrating some gross irresponsibility. The thought immediately comes to my mind that the patient will certainly fail, that this is a set up to hurt herself again, and that I have to help her be more realistic. I am tempted to say that it would be better to wait till she feels better or to attempt a less-challenging job. In the case of the patient who could not budget, I had a flash of only disastrous results when she told me she was applying for a job to keep books for a small business. I had to force myself not to hold her back. I had to remind myself that she is intelligent and capable in general and that she is setting me up to replay with her the previous experiences of being held back. At the same time, she is inducing fear in me that she herself must have about the job. It was my job to feed back that fear to her realistically and allow her growth. Her plan actually showed her pulling toward strength and autonomy in spite of the fear. I said to her, "Sounds good! I imagine you must have thought about this for a while (even if it is not likely that she did). I can see you want to do something more challenging to feel your strength. It may take a little to learn about the job, and it is a little scary, but it can be done. Let me know if I can help somehow." The help I had in mind is the kind I may have given any friend or relative, but within the office boundary. The goal of this help was to give concrete help to the best of my ability (such as sources of information, etc.) and provide experience with the parental figure who is clearly helping her to gain strength and autonomy. At no time would I do something for the patient that I know she could do for herself, such as making calls for her. At the same time, I would be there to digest for her any insecurity and fear she may have by plodding along in spite of such feelings manifesting in the both of us.

If the patient came to me with a crisis as this project was in progress, I would look at our previous recent contact or her recent contacts with the important people in her life to see if a message of abandonment had been given. This may have been from overly enthusiastic confidence in the patient or from a lack of any help given. In that case, again I would interpret her fear of being abandoned.

5. I do not usually initiate any particular topic with the patient in the session. The patient always comes up with something, even if it is their sitting silently that induces concern in me. If the patient seems to be just "chatting" and brings "no therapeutic work" to the session, I am not concerned. I see this as the patient exercising her own autonomy in my

presence and an opportunity for us to emotionally bind without pain to the patient. The only thing I may do is ask about any precipitating events before the last emotional upheaval, if that was not previously discussed.

Lastly, I do not teach skills to the patient. That seems to backfire as the patient will increasingly demonstrate an inability to solve problems on her own.

Chapter 3

Course of Therapy

As therapy progresses it is important to be aware of and prepared for certain developments. As stated in chapter 2, improvement does not occur in a steady, forward progression. Periods of great regression do occur even after a prolonged period of "benign relating" with the therapist. Many months can pass where the patient will not bid for a merger with the therapist or anyone else on the basis of the patient's pain. Crises that do occur for the patient are dealt with in a direct manner, with the patient being able to accept help without a subsequent escalation of symptoms. Things can be so good that the therapist can start thinking they were wrong about the diagnosis or congratulate themselves on the brilliant cure of this BPD patient. Yet, when a threat of abandonment occurs that is especially serious to the patient, the patient can surprise the therapist with a barrage of very self-destructive behavior and overwhelming affect.

Stage I

In the beginning, the therapist has three tasks to accomplish.

The first task is the establishment of the diagnosis. As mentioned previously, arriving at an early diagnosis of BPD is most helpful in avoiding getting caught in a downward-spiraling course. This is where the patient becomes more and more self-hurting and the therapist becomes more and more frustrated, afraid and caught in unproductive attempts to help the patient. If this does occur, it is a clue that the diagnosis considered (most likely affective disorder) is not the correct one. The diagnosis of BPD should be considered and confirmed. If, indeed, the patient has BPD as described in chapter 1 and the introduction, then the perverse relating will be evident with the therapist and the patient will give stories of repeated crises in life with some kind of self-hurting behavior always involving other people. If, at the same time, the emotional resonance with the therapist does give the patient relief, the diagnosis is confirmed and the approach to therapy can be changed. When this diagnosis is arrived at, it is good that the therapist shares with the patient in the understanding of the patient's problem. This, of course, can be done only after some historical evidence, as told by the patient, is available. Then the therapist can say, "You told me how stifled you felt when your husband took your medicines away when you talked of suicide," or "You told me how unbearable it was for you when your parents doled out your money when you overspent," or whichever story the patient related when they could not tolerate someone's saving interventions after their behavior obviously prompted this help. Then, I would proceed with saying, "It seems to me that you have suffered a lot and that you have not had much experience having anyone with you (here I put my hand on my chest) when you were feeling well and strong. That is sad and lonely. And you have mainly had people with you (hand on my chest) when you were in pain. That is also sad and not enough. As we work together, you and I may also fall into the same pattern. In the long run, it is our task to change that pattern. It is my task to be with you (again, hand on my chest) when you are also strong and well."

The second task is to establish therapy parameters. This means how often the patient will come for therapy, when and where the therapy shall take place; and what the fee shall be and how it shall be paid.

Being very clear about these parameters is more important with these patients than with some others because of the following two reasons:

The first is that, since these patients are sensitive to abandonment, they can feel abandoned just by random changes of the above parameters. Though, when this does have to occur, it can be dealt with as with any other abandonment the patient reacts to (i.e., as an opportunity to work through). Frequent changes in the parameters can also create confusion as to whether the patient is reacting to outside events or to the changes in therapy parameters. This experience of abandonment by the therapist also keeps the patient in an agitated, negative experience with the therapist, thus making the change in relating impossible at worst, and slow to develop at best.

The second reason to be very clear about the parameters is so that the therapist does not give special arrangements because the patient is in "trouble" or is "unable".

Of course, true-life situations for the therapist or the patient may demand some changes in the therapy parameters. A steady time, place, and fee will help to make those needed true-life changes easier to recognize, and, if there is a downturn for the patient after the change, it is easier to deal with.

As I have mentioned previously, because the BPD patient can be predicted to want more and more unions with the therapist when feeling bad, they are likely to call with a crisis at any time. It is thus good to clearly state what the patient should do when in a crisis between sessions.

As soon as the patient and I have been able to state that we have to learn to "be together" when she is feeling well and strong (using the patient's own experiences), I state that, if in crisis, the patient should wait for the next session to discuss it. If the patient feels that she cannot wait and is in danger, I tell her to go to the emergency room. I clarify that if she is hospitalized, I would not be the therapist there but would see her as soon as she is discharged. I state that if I did not do things that way, I would, in the long run, be hurting her. On the other hand, I say that if she just wants to have a little contact with me, or share some good news, she can call me at any time, even at three in the morning. I would be glad to hear her, though I may be sleepy and unable to talk long. This makes it clear to the patient that I truly do want to help her feel received and "be with her," not just when she is ill but also when she is well. The stage for reversing the "perverse relating" is set.

While some therapists feel that the BPD patient needs to be seen several times a week, I think that the frequency of the sessions is best tailored to the particular patient as they come.

Case 8.1

The patient has never been in therapy before and comes to therapy in crisis. It is likely that the diagnosis may not be clear at first, and initially, the sessions will be frequent: two, three, or more times per week. As soon as the diagnosis is clear and the goals are set, it is good to tell the patient that the frequency will be cut to once a week at the pre-established time by the therapist and the patient. As this is set or enacted, the patient may get even worse as they react to what they perceive as abandonment. This reaction can be handled by paying attention to the emotional resonance set up between the patient and the therapist, interpreting the patient's fear of making it alone for the duration, and slowing down the plan, but always with the view of eventually effecting the change to one session per week.

It can further help to remind the patient that they have mentioned their dislike of being held down and stifled.

Case 8.2

The patient has never had therapy and previously the crisis (or crises) has subsided as some important person in the patient's life has helped them via emotional resonance. This is unusual presentation, but it does occur. Initially, the sessions should be set to once a week. While eventually the sessions should be even less frequent, it is best to wait for the patient to initiate this change. It is also likely that the patient may happily wish to come to therapy less often, only to return in crisis a little later; this is likely because the sense of abandonment when doing well sets in. Interpreting this as follows can help: "You were so busy with your life and needed to cut down on sessions, but you may have then felt too cut-off from me. Maybe you even felt like I did not care and was just letting you go off alone." When the patient cuts down on the frequency of their sessions and seems to be doing well, it can help to say to the patient. "Sure, you are too busy and do not need to come here so often. Of course, we have been meeting once a week for so long, it will be a change. I shall worry a little about you, but only a little. See you in two weeks." This can diminish some of the fear the patient may get when, during the absence, they may feel afraid and alone.

The statements "It shall be a change," and "I shall worry a little about you. But only a little," may, if remembered by the patient, serve enough for the connection and digestion of their fear.

Case 8.3

The patient has been in therapy with someone else just before starting therapy with a different therapist. In this case it is important to find out why the patient has changed their therapist. If the therapist has died, retired, or moved away, the patient is in true crisis and should be seen more frequently at first. The task in the sessions is to provide relief of the overwhelming affect for the patient by the emotional resonance that will be set up. It is also very important to talk about the previous therapist and not to avoid the subject. This is important even if the patient is suicidal or psychotic-like, or otherwise in great emotional and mental distress, and yet denies the connection between the present turmoil and the loss of their therapist. It is the therapist's task to connect the patient's emotional state to the separation and provide words that express feelings which the patient may not be able to have. It is important to say to the patient "You must miss (insert the name of the previous therapist). I shall never take the place of him. I shall only be another person." Thus, it is possible to help the patient grieve the loss.

However, if the patient has changed therapists just because the other therapist left for vacation, or the patient became angry at the therapist for not fulfilling all their needs, the task is to help digestion of the patient's feelings via emotional resonance and send the patient back to the original therapist as soon as possible.

Case 8.4

If the patient had been in therapy for a long while and then interrupted the therapy on their own for a substantial period of time and is now in crisis, but cannot go back to the old therapist, it is wise to avoid very frequent sessions from the beginning.

This patient has probably gained much from therapy before, and the new therapist has to guard against allowing too much regression in the patient during this crisis. In this case, after the initial evaluation and diagnosis is confirmed, the frequency of sessions should be set for once every two weeks.

Case 8.5

Sometimes the patient comes right after a prolonged therapy where things have seemed to go progressively downhill. The therapist has obviously tried so hard to help, while the patient seemed to get worse and worse. They were engaged in perverse relating to the maximum. The therapist may have become so worn down that he gave up on the patient or, "luckily," had to move away. This patient now comes in great crisis, with undigested feelings of abandonment and rage, as well as an expectation that only many sessions a week will do. At the same time, this patient feels very enraged for being abandoned, despite previously being in a state of perpetual crisis just to avoid this very feeling (although they are not conscious of this).

The new therapist's instinct may dictate that they establish the same frequency and intensity of concern for the patient as the previous therapist did and then slowly cut back on the frequency of the sessions. In this case, I find that actually setting the initial session frequency to every two weeks, as soon as the diagnosis is made, is most helpful to the patient. This gives the patient "some room to breathe" as they adjust to the experience of having a new therapist. This makes sense when we remember that the BPD patient longs to be strong and well and, at the same time, not feel abandoned. The statement, "You can call when needing a contact or to share something good anytime" and the clarification of the therapeutic goal, as stated above, particularly helps these patients. Of course, they still require a lot of work during the sessions, using emotional resonance to help them digest the tremendous feelings they have at this time of change.

The third task for stage I of the therapy is to be consciously aware of how the beginning of therapy will unfold.

During this beginning period of work with the BPD patient, it will be noticed that the patient comes with demonstrations or descriptions of their emotional distress. They do not connect it to any events outside of themselves. They are very happy to accept that they have a "chemical problem" or some kind of "mental illness." The "paranoid schizophrenic" who insists and argues that he is indeed a paranoid schizophrenic is usually a patient with BPD. When listening to these patients describe their emotional suffering, it can be noted that they mainly convey extreme affects such as horrendous despair or rage. They convey the feeling, but not how they got here. They experience these extreme, debilitating feelings as if in a partially preverbal state. They do not use words such as "abandonment," "hopelessness," "utter loneliness," "despair," and so on. As they have difficulty identifying the events that preceded the affect, they cannot say, for example, "My boyfriend left town, and I feel terribly abandoned, uncared for, and lost. I cannot exist without him." It is the therapist's job to patiently inquire about the life situation and events just before the overwhelming emotional episode. While we may ask a general question such as "What happened that you are so upset?" chances are the patient will say "nothing" or "I do not know." It is better to ask more specific questions that will enable us, as therapists, to reconstruct the events that led to the emotional decompensation of the patient. Thus, asking about who the patient lives with, where they were when they got upset, who did or said what, who they showed their pain to, and so on, will be more productive.

Even when asking specific questions about the events, the patient may not be able to respond while in the middle of tremendous emotional crisis. They need relief of their overwhelming, painful affect before they can respond much to the therapist. It is imperative to remember that the therapist's first task is to relieve them of such pain. It is important to remember that we have to wait and let the patient express the affect, with whatever means they wish, and that, first, the therapist must feel the patient's feelings before the patient can start feeling relieved. When the patient starts calming down, then the questions about events can be answered and a story can unfold.

This story unfolds for the therapist first. The therapist puts it together and tells it to the patient. The patient will most likely not accept it right away, but the patient *will* seem calmer. This is because, via emotional resonance, they are receiving our calmer handling of the feeling. In the meantime, we are setting the basis for the development of more mature and more grounding mental processes for the patient, allowing them to make sense of what has happened to them.

This first stage of therapy is usually quite long. The duration depends on whether the patient was in therapy before and how the therapy went, the patient's life circumstances, and their previous functions in jobs, and so forth. Years can go by with the same manner of relating while the crisis (or crises) mainly becomes less frequent or changes only in its form. One patient moved from taking pill overdoses, to cutting herself superficially, to scratching herself, to talking of driving the car over the bridge, to drinking alcohol, to talking in detail about funeral arrangements, and so on. The greatest movement in this stage is the patient's ability to recount life events preceding the crisis, although they may still not be able to state that the feelings resulted from the events.

Stage II

After a prolonged time when the patient relates mainly via the perverse relating mode, cannot connect feelings to events well, and uses splitting and emotional resonance mainly to survive their overwhelming feelings, some changes can be observed that signal a new stage of therapy is happening. These changes occur episodically and definitely not consistently. These changes, while signifying a maturing of the patient and definite improvement, will at first also confuse the therapist as to how now to proceed with therapy.

The patient has not had a crisis for a while. This always lulls the therapist into forgetting that a resolve was made not to show too much joy to the patient when they have talked of a particularly successful endeavor. This "lulling and forgetting" by the therapist is an important symptom of progress. The therapist shows joy over this success. The patient, who always responded by getting worse after a session when some praise or joy was shown by the therapist, now seems to beam when this happens and may even express some self-satisfaction with their own achievement or growth. The patient does not automatically take back any self-confirmation, and the joyful experience of strength and well-being is not followed by crisis in the next session.

This change in the session may not be noted by the therapist until after a few sessions have passed and no crisis has occurred. Often the therapist goes through this experience almost "unconsciously." But the therapist who might have dreaded the sessions with the patient (because they have anticipated a crisis) starts looking forward to them. At this point, the therapist becomes aware that this was not just a pause in crises but a change in relating. The relating is now comfortable. Accordingly, the therapist thinks the approach to the patient must change; there is no longer a need to pay much attention to emotional resonance. The next time a crisis occurs, the therapist does not consciously digest the feelings for the patient but only shows empathy, such as "You felt so bad," or gives suggestions for relief, such as new medication. This almost always fails, and the therapist has to go back to paying attention to the emotional resonance the patient is setting up and still requires. Thus, I think of this stage of therapy as the "flexibility is a must" stage. This is the stage when the therapist is challenged intellectually more than emotionally. It is also the most interesting stage.

Some common themes will come up for the patients, specifically the following:

1. The awareness of the merger
2. Awareness of how the merger is set up
3. Connection between life events and the crisis is incomplete and lags in time
4. Appearance of guilt and sorrow
5. Exaggerated sense of guilt
6. Developing the ability to remember crises and resolutions over time

1. The Awareness of the Merger

Patients express this awareness of merger more and more clearly as therapy progresses. During the crises, which still occur (although less often), the patient spontaneously tries to find words for the merging experience. One patient described in detail how she experienced her husband watching her after she very clearly told him she will kill herself. "He is watching me all the time. I cannot stand it. I feel I have no air to breathe. I cannot stand to even sleep in the same room with him. Even seeing his things on the kitchen counter makes me feel he is too much there. Like his things are intruding. I just need to be alone a bit. He is stifling! That is it, he is stifling me! Funny, I did not feel this way about him just last week." During the time she described this, she did not feel suicidal as she had felt during the week she was talking about.

Another patient would fax me letters and poems filled with despair and suicidal threats, and then come to the sessions saying nothing about these unless I brought it up. She said, "I had a funny dream. I dreamt that you were angry and said to me 'you are making me feel like you, think like you, decide for you!' I know this is not true. When I write things to you, I feel you are doing that to me. You are controlling me. I need some privacy from you." Yet, most of the time, I say nothing about these communications until the end of sessions when it is obvious that she will say nothing. I know that if *I* say absolutely nothing, the emotional resonance between us will not work, and she will get lost in the feelings and might hurt herself. I usually say something like "I got your letter. I could feel how bad you are feeling." This seemed sufficient to calm her and encourage her to experience a merger with me.

2. *Awareness of How the Merger Is Set Up*

Patients become more able and willing to examine what their role was in getting to the situation of feeling stifled. Previously, the fact that they evoke what they feel are stifling responses in others is out of their awareness. The patient who complained about her husband was able to spontaneously say, "I know he worried about me when I told him I will kill myself, but he just becomes too much!"

The patient who accused me of controlling her said, "I know you say so little and that I am the one who writes you the letters."

At these moments of insight, the patients seem to develop some intellectual curiosity about how they have provoked the responses which make them feel stifled, and they will often talk at length about this. Now is the opportunity to examine and define what this merger feeling is like, when it occurs, how they bring it on, and how they want it at first and hate it later. The patient with the husband could tell, without prompting, exactly what she said to the husband before he started watching her. The patient who wrote letters actually came to the next session stating that she thought about the previous conversation and decided that she "goes fishing" with her letters for my response. She also said that she does similar things with other people and then does not like their concern. It was clear to her that what she writes or says invites people to be very concerned about her, think a lot about her, and "feel."

It is important to note that these patients developed these realizations without any prompting or leading on my part. All that I did was examine the situations before an emotional upheaval and attempt to name the feelings that may be underneath the total despair and rage.

This developing awareness and ability to use verbalization is a great step forward in the development of an awareness of self without total emotional flooding. It also shows that the patients are finding intellectualization comforting. It is interesting to see that, as the patients get relief of the overwhelming affects via emotional resonance, they spontaneously adopt more mature mechanisms of defense and do not hang on to "splitting."

3. *Connection between Life Events and the Crisis Is Incomplete and Lags in Time*

It must noted that the awareness of this merger and how it comes about does not always mean that the patient is aware of what precipitates the initial emotional crisis that propels them to evoke the "stifling" responses of others. At the beginning of therapy, if the therapist asks "What happened before you started feeling this way?" the patient is likely to say "nothing," or "I don't remember." In time, the patient is better able to recall events, first with the therapist's prodding and, later, even spontaneously. However, often they cannot put how they felt as the result of the upsetting events into words, except to describe the self-hurting behavior or fantasies. This is because the overwhelming affect after the events is indeed "indescribable" for them for a long time. They cannot say, for example, "I felt so rejected, alone, and afraid when my husband said he was going on the trip." They only talk of the suicidal ideation, and so on. The work of naming the feelings for the patient after an upsetting event remains with the therapist for a long time. Eventually, the patient no longer denies the connections when the therapist points them out. The patient even seems relieved when the therapist gives words to such feelings as abandonment, panic of being rejected, fear of total aloneness, and others.

In the next step, the patient starts to consistently talk of events before the turmoil. But the patient still needs the therapist to name the feelings associated with the events for a long time, despite the consistent, spontaneous recollection of the upsetting events. It is only when the abandonment feeling is not so horrendous that the patient can say, as one did, "My daughter left on vacation without telling me . . . You know how that made me feel . . . like I did not matter . . . I lost her . . . so I went to bed and couldn't do anything for a whole day." She was able to tolerate the feeling on her own and did not involve me or anyone else to help her with it.

4. *Appearance of Guilt and Sorrow*

As the patient begins to realize that they have set up the other person's "stifling" behavior toward them, they also become aware that the response of this person (or persons) was actually intended to help them. This awareness shows their ability to acknowledge the other person's good and bad aspects (i.e., the helping aspects and the "stifling" aspects). The patient is now integrating the emotional concepts they have of that person.

As mentioned before in this book, the patient now experiences guilt. This guilt is expressed by statements such as "I feel I am putting you in an impossible situation," or "I feel I am putting so much pressure on my husband that he does not know what to do," or "How can you stand me!"

Sometimes the guilt is expressed through reparative action. One patient, after a particularly difficult episode with me (an episode which was also difficult on me), brought a pot of chicken soup and left it in the waiting room with a note, "Because you have a cold, you should have canceled our appointment and taken care of yourself." I considered the soup and her note as tremendous improvement for that patient. It demonstrated that she was integrated about her feelings about me: she felt guilty for hurting me whom she also loved. She knew how to use reparation to assuage her guilt: the gift of soup. She demonstrated that she knew I was not simply a horrible, unfeeling therapist but was actually someone who was there for her. She was able to feel empathy for me suffering from a cold. She further acted on this empathy with the selfless statement that I should have taken care of myself and not her at that time. Most important of all: where was the fear of abandonment? She could actually conceive of a situation where I was caring for myself and not in the office for her without feeling abandoned. Of course, this all occurred after her crisis was over and after I was there to help her digest her feelings. If I had not been there, she would have been in an escalating crisis until I came back. Nevertheless, this was a vast improvement in this patient who, years beforehand, had absolutely no ability for any of the described responses. For a long time, she was oblivious as to how she made me feel.

The theme of guilt, reparation, and sorrow is a very important one to work on, for it strengthens the patient's integration of the disparate feeling aspects of themselves and others. This becomes possible as the disparate feelings lose their strength and the splitting is no longer needed defensively. At the same time, the mending of the split itself (the good that can be remembered diminishes the bad that is experienced) brings down the strength of the disparate feelings. It is, at this point, that reminding the patient of their disparate feelings about people can help the mending of the split and lead to integration. In the first stage of the therapy, however, mentioning these disparate feeling perceptions to the patient does not help much. Now, when the therapist points out the disparate feelings the patient had, the patient can sometimes say with feeling, "Yes, I know."

As these integrations occur, it becomes even clearer that the patient never had the intent to hurt us and make us feel as we did. The unconscious intent was only to get us to help them digest the overwhelming affect. This became very clear after the last emotional resonance a patient set up with me. After a long time of what I call "nonperverse" relating with me, she came to a session, talking again about planning to kill herself. I approached the session as I had been. As we got up at the end of the sessions, she said to me, "Now that we talked, I feel sure that my plan to end it all is correct." As usual, I said to her, "I feel bad that I could not help you more. If anything, I made you feel worse." Variations on this theme had happened multiple times before, with her leaving without saying anything: leaving me to hold the fear and the feeling of total, disastrous ineffectiveness. But, this time, she immediately said, "Oh! No. Don't feel that! You don't know how much you help me!" She had no intention to make me feel bad, although her statements would make anyone have the same feelings as I did. Her intent was only to use me to relieve *herself*. The moment she felt better, this time, she became aware of me as an individual (i.e., separate from her) and wished to soothe me. Previously, she was not able to see me as being more than just an emotional crutch.

5. Exaggerated Sense of Guilt

The guilt I have talked about in the paragraphs above is the guilt that arose after the patient became aware of the merger they have set up and their responses to this awareness. However, these patients also seem to experience a sense of tremendous guilt at the beginning of their crisis. It seems that this is one of the first statements they can make about what they feel in response to the life events that have led to the tremendous affective crisis.

The sequence is actually that the patient first feels abandoned by an important person in their life. This triggers an horrendous separation anxiety and rage in response to being abandoned. The rage is experienced as a total loss of control and a desire to destroy the existence of the other while effecting the merger. This is sometimes acted out by furious verbal attacks at the "abandoning" one or by furious rejection of the abandoning one while not letting the abandoning one go. Sometimes, although it is rare, this is also acted out physically (e.g., a hospitalized patient accused the staff of not letting him go and threw a chair across the room when he was told he was being discharged). As the patient becomes better able to tolerate less guilt over being angry for being "stifled" or abandoned, they also become better able to recognize themselves as extremely bad/evil as they perceive themselves destroying the one they do not wish to lose. Initially, this cannot be put in words, and it is quickly lost as the merger occurs. Once the merger occurs, there is no longer the sense of abandonment or the rage over it. There is only the need to get rid of the stifling merger. As patients get better, they are able to get in touch with this sense of being evil. They usually call this guilt. It is the awareness of destroying, not the one they love, but the one they need. This is experienced by us—by all of humanity—as the greatest of evils.

We can all attest to the fact that when these patients ask us to help them and then say or demonstrate that we actually hurt them with our help, we do feel that we are hurtful: we become evil therapists. The digested feeling we have to give back to them is usually a sense of being unwillingly hurtful to the patient and unable to stop this hurtfulness while we actually desire so much the opposite—the way they feel.

Case 9.1

A patient became very suicidal and regressed when somebody in church expressed the opinion that mental illness is possession by the devil. Though she is quite intelligent and knew this was not so, she felt directly accused. She was not able to defend herself in any way. She began talking and doing things that made people around her feel, unwittingly, very evil. She sent an anonymous e-mail to the minister of the church, not explaining what had happened, but making it clear that because his church is hurting her, she will kill herself.

She desperately needed help in tolerating this sense of being evil and eventually used the emotional resonance she set up with others successfully. This patient experienced this at the time when she was able to tolerate some sense of guilt but not yet able to talk about it. Years later, she told the story of totally losing herself in screams, accusations, and of pushing her mother away, shortly before she had to move far away from her. Though she was moving away from her mother, she experienced tremendous separation anxiety and felt the mother was abandoning her. The patient then became able to identify feeling "very guilty" as she fell into one of her emotional crises. Her usual suicidal ideas, however, did not represent self-punishment but rather a bid for merger. It was also easily demonstrated that an event would occur when she felt first rejected and abandoned, then became panicked, then enraged, then "evil," and then the suicidal ideation would occur. There was no relief if she did hurt herself, such as scraping her arms with a knife, until she told someone about this and made them feel "evil." She became aware that the feelings she had before becoming suicidal were much worse than when she was suicidal. She could describe periods of lying in bed and constantly fantasizing of hurting herself and that her family would know how evil they were after her death. She never fantasized that they would feel repentant and sorry that she died. That was not the point. It was not to punish them but to make them feel as she did.

The task for the therapist is to help the patient reframe this sense of being "evil" as, instead, rage for being abandoned. It also helps to put into words that the patient is not really wishing to destroy the one they need but rather trying to destroy the sense that they are separate, that they are trying to merge. It can also help to point out that, sometimes, we all need someone in our lives who we know will not abandon us and with whom we can feel "one" with. It is important to remember that, occasionally, the patient will still need the therapist to digest this sense of being "evil" via emotional resonance.

6. *Developing the Ability to Remember Crises and Resolutions over Time*

As previously mentioned, for a long time, at first, the patient behaves as if the emotional crisis at hand is the only thing they can remember. This is because they are so overwhelmed by the affect that they cannot attend to the past or the future. Because of this, at first, it may be difficult for patients to give a good history of what preceded the emotional crisis. They cannot recall that they have had similar crises in the past and that these crises did resolve, and that the present one can also be expected to resolve. This is something the therapist has to recall for them time and again.

In the second stage of therapy, the patient may say, "This is the worst I have ever felt," or "Every time I feel bad it is worse than before." This indicates that the patient is able to recall that previous crises did occur and that the present one is not so bad that it blocks any ability to remember.

The patient in case 9.1 was, at the same time, able to temporize the execution of her plan to die and said, "I am giving myself two weeks before I go."

My only response was to reinforce her ability to conceive of freedom from the overwhelming affect. I said, "I too can remember that in the past, you felt like this and then, after a while, you felt better." I did not argue with her that this crisis is not worse than before. Her statement was to convey the seriousness of her plight now: to involve me in the emotional resonance with her and to induce in me the fear, responsibility, impotence, guilt, and anger, which she felt.

Stage III

In time, there is a greater sense of comfort and confidence on the part of the therapist that therapy can proceed without paying attention to the emotional resonance the patient may induce. Periods without enormous emotional crises become longer and longer. This does not mean that the patient does not have times when she feels bad, but that the quality of these upheavals is different. The therapist does not feel the urgency to relieve the patient immediately. The patient can name feelings like feeling rejected, sad, guilty, ashamed, and so on. There is definitely the sense that the patient's emotion is dampened by her verbalization.

The patient is also able to consistently share positive plans and feelings without any decompensation afterward. There is almost a feeling of exhilaration that the patient is able to share with and, at times, induce in the therapist. This is equivalent to the mother feeling exhilarated when her small child accomplishes something and takes the child into a heartfelt embrace.

In essence, the perverse relating has been abandoned, and the patient can now pick up on the separation-individuation work she has been trying to complete all those years. She is not stuck in fear that her ventures into strength and individuation will lead into abandonment. She can actually feel reinforcement of herself via the temporary sense of union with the therapist. The feelings are no longer overwhelming. If separation anxiety occurs, it can be soothed without annihilation of the patient's individuation—without the merger—but with the mere presence of the therapist.

It is important to recognize this change in the relating of the patient so that the therapist can facilitate the patient's maturation. Some of the differences in approach are described in the remainder of this chapter.

1. It would be detrimental if the therapist now uses the approach initially used to focus on the patient's fears about their plans to accomplish something. Initially the response should have always covered the patient's desire to do well alongside their fear about the endeavor.

    Statements might have been, "Sounds good! You may have some fear that you cannot do this. I too have some concerns, but I think you can work it out." Now, the statement should not mention fear. The patient does not need the therapist to digest the fear for her. It can be simply "Sounds neat! Tell me all about it." The patient may very well express some trepidation about the endeavor. All the therapist needs to do is say something like, "I understand." Exploration of the plan can be direct and straightforward, with the therapist only asking factual questions and contributing factual information. Sharing enthusiasm can be expressed freely.

2. The patient now no longer needs the therapist to digest insupportable, negative feelings for her.

    If the patient brings in the story of something unpleasant having happened, the therapist can express sorrow, point out injustices, and even say, "How terrible!" The therapist may still have to name some feelings that one could have under the circumstances. However, the therapist is not called upon to resonate the affects only. It is not necessary to say, "I see how bad you feel. I too feel bad that I cannot help more." The therapist is called upon to show true empathy. Understanding how the patient feels is what is needed now, and not just feeling the same feelings as the patient.

3. The patient is able to recall past life experiences more accurately.

    It is often remarkable to me to hear a different story about the patient's mother, in particular. In the beginning, the patient usually describes the mother as a very hurtful person. If the patient does talk of good interactions with the mother, these seem to be totally isolated from the bad experiences. Now, however, the patient can say something like "My mother said terrible things about me, but she always took up my side when I was in trouble in school." This demonstrates an ability to see the mother both as bad and good at the same time. While initially, in therapy, pointing out or recounting good and bad experiences with the mother would either be useless or result in the patient becoming angry, this is now a very helpful technique. The patient will begin to lose the image of their mother being extremely evil to them. While some mothers may have actually been extremely bad at times and extremely good at times, more often it comes out in therapy at this stage that the mother was never extremely evil. This is because the patient's image of her evilness has now been modified by the patient's ability to bring in the image of the "good mother." The extremely evil mother seems to disappear for the patient. Patients can now be encouraged to talk more about their childhood experiences. They are also able to look at the parents who themselves have had life experiences that helped form them. One of my patients was finally able to say, "No wonder my mother was like that. Her mother died when she was small and her father was abusive." In the beginning of therapy, the patient may have the motto "I am the way I am because my mother was mean to me." Now the patient can engage in realistic evaluations of how her experiences may have affected her specifically. She can also tolerate and should be helped to see her own part in "how mother acted with her." Part of this examination includes examination of how the patient is the same and how she is different from the mother. This last is very helpful in strengthening individuation.

4. Many patients with BPD give histories of physical or sexual abuse. Usually, concentrating on these issues in the beginning of therapy is not helpful.

The patient and the therapist often get embroiled in ever-escalating exploration and reliving of the trauma with escalating self-hurting behavior by the patient. This is usually interpreted as the patient finally being in touch with the feelings around the trauma and that, in time, the patient will "work through" the feelings. Actually, even these memories can serve the patient to achieve mergers with the therapist via self-hurting. Once the patient has been able to tolerate strong feelings without the use of emotional resonance with the therapist, the patient now becomes better equipped to deal with the abusive traumas. Sometimes these traumas, when re-examined later, lose the horrendous qualities they initially had for the patient. Sometimes the patient goes on in life, much better adjusted, without ever bringing up the traumas again. Sometimes the patient denies that they have occurred. The therapist must be prepared for any eventuality about these remembered traumas. It must be understood that less emotional turmoil, better interpersonal relations, and beneficial work adjustment is the actual goal for the patient and not the process of "working through the trauma" as in our preconceived manner.

Even when the patient seems to have achieved the abilities described above, there can always be setbacks. The patient can suddenly have another presentation in severe crisis when it is obvious that the therapist is again called upon to digest the feelings for the patient via patient-evoked emotional resonance. This occurs when there is a very serious rejection or abandonment by a very significant person in her life. The therapist must be prepared for these occurrences that would now come as surprises. Reverting back to the initial approaches to the patient does help. The patient usually recovers from this crisis easier and sooner. Spiraling down does not occur, and progress can pick up again.

Chapter 4

Inpatient Treatment

There is controversy as to the helpfulness of an inpatient stay for people with BPD. Historically, it has been claimed that these patients are both better and worse after a long hospitalization. I think this is because the different patients were exposed to different types of treatment in various hospitals. They re-enact the perverse relating and try to work out separation-individuation with the hospital staff. They respond to the act of hospitalization, per se, as an act of merger and loss of individuality. How the staff responds to this need is what determines whether the patient benefits from the hospitalization or becomes more reinforced in their pathology.

Usually BPD patients are hospitalized during a serious crisis. Once in, they tend to give up all control into the hands of the staff and, at the same time, are very angry for being controlled. As they threaten self-injury, they, of course, provoke the staff to watch them carefully and restrict their "privileges." Now the patient complains of being controlled but continues to exhibit threatening self-injury behavior. The staff escalates the vigil of protection and a downhill cycle ensues. The worst example of this was in a state hospital inpatient unit where the resources were only enough for basic protection and medication. After a whole year in the hospital, one of these patients ended up escalating his self-injury from initially using medicine overdoses to cutting his throat multiple times. The fact that these patients seem to "regress" in the hospital is well recognized. Because of this, the staff on units are usually wary of these patients and seek to discharge them as soon as possible. This discharge usually happens when the patient has been observed by staff to be in a quite good mood with other patients and has also annoyed the staff by complaints of their control. Often, soon after such a discharge, the patient is seen in the emergency unit, very seriously suicidal, and is readmitted. Now the inpatient staff and the admitting staff are in opposite corners, often thinking the other does not know what they are doing and are mistreating the patient or are being manipulated by the patient. The truth is that the patient was both in serious emotional crisis in front of the admitting staff and truly ready for freedom in front of the hospital staff. This switch happened in the patient. The patient first needed the emotional container and the merger of hospitalization; soon, however, the patient came to experience this merger as invasive and required the freedom.

To get out of this bind about hospitalization of these patients, I recommend that the staff be aware of the meaning of the act of "taking over" for these patients that hospitalization represents. A long hospitalization, preferably not initiated during a crisis for the patient, where the patient is systematically afforded opportunities to work out the separation-individuation task, can be very helpful. The opportunity for long hospitalization is rare in our current economic situation. Lacking this opportunity, I recommend that hospitalization of these patients be as short as possible, with a very systematic therapeutic use of their regressive merging reactions to the hospitalization. Any in-between attempt in the hospitalization of these patients is usually disastrous, with the patient often being shipped off on a commitment to someplace else.

I am going to describe now what I mean by "systematic therapeutic use of the patient's regressive merging reactions to the hospitalization."

1. The patient is hospitalized in a serious crisis—usually suicidal. The people on the unit—patients and staff—become partners in the emotional resonance the patient sets up. If there is enough "being upset with the patient without being panicked," the patient will experience some soothing of her feelings.

    1. As soon as this is seen, I tell the patient that all their emotional problems will not be solved by the hospital. I tell them they may actually end up feeling worse in the hospital. Optimal therapy for them is in an outpatient setting. This is a true and empathic statement to the patient, who indeed gets to feel too controlled by the staff.
    2. I discuss outpatient therapy with them and take steps for referral. If possible, I arrange for the first meeting with the new outpatient therapist while the patient is in the hospital. This therapist should not be a member of the hospital staff. If the patient already has

an outpatient therapist, I do not encourage visits by this therapist while the patient is still in the hospital. I try to find out whether the patient experienced a sense of abandonment by the therapist (such as vacation, rejection, etc.). I only empathize with how the patient must have felt. I do tell the patient that I shall be in touch with the therapist and shall set up the next appointment if she does not have one already within the week of discharge.
   3. I ask the patient to think when the date of discharge shall be and to tell me this on a certain (specified by me) day. I anticipate in my mind a stay of only a few days or a couple of weeks, depending on how serious their "abandonment" was and what support they have outside the hospital.

2. On the day the patient is to tell me when the discharge shall be, the patient may have had another episode of suicidal crisis or simply have not set a date of discharge.

   1. I interpret this as her fear of leaving the hospital and making it alone.
   2. I point out that this is similar to other times in her life when she had separations, such as just before she came to the hospital. (By that time I have some historical data as to the events just before the patient came.)
   3. I repeat that hospitalizations can make her feel worse, and I cite any hints of this that she may have shown by complaints or negative reactions in the hospital. I also repeat our plans for the outpatient therapy.
   4. I am conscious of the emotional resonance the patient is setting up, and I act as described in the previous section.
   5. Again, I invite the patient to set the discharge date, and if she cannot do so at the time of this conversation, I set the date of discharge myself. If the patient argues, I repeat that outpatient therapy is better for her and that by keeping her long in the hospital, I would be hurting her.

3. If the patient comes up with a very precipitous date for discharge, such as "now," I interpret this also as fear of separation.
   I say she may be throwing herself out in order not to face the fear. I say I will worry about her, and I try to postpone the discharge by a day. But I also say that I will not force her to stay.

4. If, on the set day of discharge, the patient acts out with a threat or some hurtful behavior, I again interpret this as fear of making it alone and tie it with the separation just before the hospitalization.

   1. I again recount any complaints she had about the hospital or negative reactions as evidence of her need for autonomy and for feeling strong and well. Any of her demands for privileges, wishes not to attend meetings, and most of the against-the-rules behavior I interpret as her need for autonomy. I point out that being in the hospital would squelch that healthy striving in her. I say that I too am worried about her leaving, but I side with the part of her that needs to feel strong and is strong. In other words, I am also participating in the emotional resonance she sets up.
   2. I postpone the date of discharge by a few days, but I state very clearly that I am doing that only once; otherwise, I would be hurting her and holding her from doing for herself and doing well.

5. If, on the day of discharge, the patient again repeats the emotional crisis, I discharge her with the same interpretation and insistence that by holding her in the hospital, I would be hurting her in the long run.

   1. I repeat all of the above observations of her striving for autonomy, and I also acknowledge that she must be very afraid of leaving. I sate that I, too, am afraid for her, but I also know that she has the ability to do well. I state again that I am very much on the side of her, who wants freedom and strength.
   2. I also make it clear that the patient can come back into the hospital immediately and make sure she knows where the admitting office or emergency room is. It is interesting that with this approach I have seen much less immediate re-hospitalization than compared to the usual discharge approach.

6. If the patient does return immediately, I approve the act as her arranging for more help.

   I make sure that I act my part in the emotional resonance she sets up, but I also act as if this is a continuation of the initial hospitalization and proceed with the same discharge plan.

7. If the patient wants to leave before the date set, I argue that this is again separation fear. I repeat that I am worried, but I also know she can do fine, and I discharge the patient.

Everything in the above plan is based on making sure that

1. I relieve the patient of the overwhelming affect by accepting the same in me and not acting precipitously or conveying panic or rage. The statements such as "I worry too" help to achieve this.
2. I never take over any decision about the patient without inviting her input. If I did, even though she acts as if she wants me to make decisions, and it may seem that she needs me to do so, she would very quickly feel stifled by this sort of unilateral decision. She would have experienced a merger. On the other hand, if I let her make the important decisions alone, she will very quickly feel afraid, abandoned, and panicked. Even my initial invitation that the patient should decide when she wants to be discharged includes my participation, just by telling her to do so.
3. Information about the events before the patient's crisis must be obtained in order to help the patient have a more intellectual comprehension of what happened that evoked the emotional crisis in her. This is an important step in helping her bring the overwhelming emotion down to a more manageable level. This also sets up a background for continual work on an outpatient basis. Often, the patient has no ability to put into words what happened and how it made her feel. She usually presents only with the symptoms and signs of severe depression or discontrol of rage, and sometimes she will even present with psychotic symptoms. In the short-term hospitalization setting we may have become misdirected into thinking that the patient has depression, psychosis, and so on. When we treat the patient for such problems per se, we lose the opportunity to help that patient diminish the affective state. We also run the risk of cycling through and escalating their symptoms and the intensity of our help. We are "treating the headache but not the cause of it."

The above approach arose from observation of a young man with BPD, who had been committed to the State Hospital from an acute voluntary hospital, where he could not stop threatening suicide. The State Hospital unit at that time was under great pressure to cut down on beds. The staff were very busy, and the beds were mainly available only to very psychotic patients. The BPD patient calmed down on that unit relatively quickly. He was given a day before discharge. On that day, he became enraged, yelling and claiming that we, the therapists on duty, did not want to let him go. As we were saying good-bye, he threw a chair across the room. The staff and the patient were in a bind since we, the therapists, were discharging him, yet he was yelling that we were not and behaved in such a way that usually we would not discharge him. Because of the pressure for beds and because he was yelling that he wished to leave, we gave him some medication to calm him down, and we discharged him. He did not come back for a few months. We realized that his whole emotionality during the discharge was based on a fear of going out and that, as we overcame our own fear, he was able to do well for a while. We found out that he never did get outpatient follow-up but did well for several months. This patient continued to have several hospitalizations to the same unit with progressively longer periods of time of being out. The staff learned to verbalize his fear of being discharged and the preparation for his discharge included many empathic statements relating to that fear. The staff also kept in mind that, originally, he was yelling that we did not want to let him go, yet he also did actually want to leave. His discharges became progressively less tumultuous. His last hospitalization was a year after the previous one, evidently having done well for the entire year. At his last discharge, he said, very appropriately, good-bye, stating that he was afraid and would miss us but also that he had to go. We found out that this patient always did better out of the hospital than we would have predicted by his presentation in the hospital, and he never did get any outpatient treatment in-between the hospitalizations. Therefore, we believe that he was working out separation-individuation issues just with the act of hospitalization followed by discharge.

Thus, I do not hospitalize my outpatient patients myself, although I do tell them that they can go to the emergency room or be hospitalized if they feel they should do so. When I worked on the inpatient units, I never took any of the BPD patients who had been hospitalized in my unit as my outpatients.

When working in the emergency room, I find that the above principles about talking to the BPD patient in crisis also help. Often, paying attention to the emotional resonance with the patient, taking time with her, and always sharing the decision about hospitalization, leads into the patient not being hospitalized and leaving, feeling better. There are situations when the patient just sits in front of the emergency room staff, not talking, and emitting "vibes of being in severe danger of suicide." She refuses to say anything when invited to give an opinion about hospitalization, and the staff feel they must hospitalize her. I then say, "I see that you cannot say anything about whether you need to go into the hospital. I sense how bad you feel. With this silence, I therefore feel that you are making me speak out your decision to be hospitalized. When you get on the unit, you will have the chance to make more verbal decisions." With this statement, I am still "sitting on the border" with the patient about taking over for her and letting her have freedom of self.

Chapter 5

Extended Interpersonal Systems

The BPD patient interacts in the same manner with anyone around who may be able and willing to digest the feelings with them and serve as a partner for the separation-individuation work they need and will, unfortunately, set up in a perverse manner. Their attempt to work out the separation-individuation task, because of the perverse relating, is doomed to fail. They cannot stay individuated as long as they perceive individuation as being abandoned as an emotionally weak infant. On the other hand, they hate the merger which helps with the denial of separateness and, thus, the possibility of abandonment but also makes them feel suffocated and kept down. They can never stay in the individuated strong state long enough to withstand the abandonment, for they do not have enough inner strength to do so. In order to be able to tolerate the abandonment, they must have the consolidation of individuation via the security of mergers when they are doing well, which is something they have not experienced much and cannot trust to happen. Thus, a cycle is set up that, by its nature, does not allow for the building of the strong individuated state. Likewise, the overwhelming affects they feel (fear and rage) do not allow for any "emotional remembering" of the presence of the good merging person which would allow for the tolerance of being a separate, lone, person. They cannot retain the emotional memory of the presence of the "good one." Their struggle is ever-present and, thus, they will turn to various people in their lives for help.

Because of this, it is important for the therapist to understand that the patient may have different presentations with other people around than with the therapist. Only when all interpersonal interactions are changed can one say that the patient has truly changed. It is because of these different presentations that people around a person with BPD will be at odds with one another as to what the problem is or what the patient needs. It is thus said that the patient "splits" people around them. It is important to remember that this does not happen because the patient wants others to fight about them; rather, it happens because the patient truly is different at different points of time and with different people. Most of the times, the same changes will eventually occur with the same people if they have long-enough contact with the patient. Thus, family and friends will eventually get the same impression about the patient. Usually they come to the point of being so exasperated by the patient that they start rejecting the patient. They abandon the patient in reality, or emotionally, because they are unable to tolerate further emotional turbulence.

It is usually the friends that will sever their relationship with these patients, eventually, totally. They usually get caught in ever-increasing threats by the BPD person that she will kill herself. They feel hostage to the patient, feeling that they must get away yet also being certain that the friend will kill herself if they do so. Some stay in the relationship until someone else intervenes and extricates them, and some end up having emotional problems themselves before they give up. There are those who learn to straddle the emotional fence of being upset with the patient but only to a certain degree. These friends will continue with the relationship and are actually very helpful to the patient. It is observed that even without much direct therapy, these patients will become more stable as they get older. It is likely that this happens because of such friendly, helpful interactions over a long period of time.

A second group of people around the BPD person are those in various helping positions: teachers, counselors, ministers, doctors, nurses, therapists, and so on. As stated before, these people can, unknowingly, easily fall into disagreement (splitting) among themselves as to what is best for the patient. One of them may give totally opposite advice to the patient from another without being aware of the discrepancy. Or they may be aware of the discrepancy but feel so convinced of their "correct" position that they openly tell the patient not to listen to the other advisor. This can, of course, cause havoc, but more so for the caregivers than the patient who will continue to go to various helpers, knowing that they give disparate advice. When we think that the patient does represent herself differently to the various helpers because she is in a different emotional state, it is not surprising that this will happen. She is getting what she needs at the time from each disparate helper.

I was asked to consult on a patient who had, in essence, five therapists. She saw a psychiatrist who saw her as psychotically depressed with the possibility of schizophrenia, a therapist who saw her as chronically suicidal because of abuse in the past, a nurse who saw her as mainly obese but otherwise well and took walks with her, two group therapists who thought of her mainly as a manipulator, and a physician who saw her as a victim of fumbling therapists who were mishandling her. In a way, I as the consultant was to be the sixth therapist to have an opinion about her. I was aware that I should not come up with yet another different opinion about her. My task, instead, was to talk to all persons involved (which I'll collectively refer to as "therapists" from here on) and point out that each opinion was correct. The therapists became aware of the different presentations the patient showed to each and that the composite was the "true" patient. Each therapist was responding to a particular presentation, which helped the patient at the moment, but did not help the patient connect these aspects of herself into one whole and did not help her in changing her perverse relating or diminish her negative affective states.

There are some principles worth remembering about the interpersonal environment of the BPD patient.

1. They always exist in a milieu with other people besides the therapist. Because they have unfinished business with the separation-individuation task, they seek people around them more than other patients do. The separation-individuation task cannot be accomplished alone.
2. Any person around them can serve the purpose of working on the separation-individuation. Unfortunately, this is done via the perverse relating that the patient sets up. Normally the partner in this relating will react by falling into the trap of becoming available to the patient more and more when they are in crisis and less and less when they are doing well.
3. The individuals involved in this perverse relating are caught in ever-escalating fears and frustration with the patient. Something has to happen eventually, and this is usually abandonment of the patient (which is actually the patient's most feared event). Sometimes a balance is established and the same interactions go on ad infinitum. Sometimes there is an instinctive, gradual response by the partner that leads to a change of the perverse relating and, ultimately, growth of the patient.

4. The patient always makes people around them fight about them. They are excellent in making the therapist feel criticized by others, be angry at others, and blame others for the patient's problems.
5. Therapy goes best when all the people involved have the understanding that their disparate views of the patient are actually a result of the patient's disparate presentations. Ultimately, when the patient narrows down to perverse relating with only one person, their growth can be sped up. This person is usually the therapist. However, I have seen where a parent became most helpful in this change and growth.

Approach to the Therapeutic Systems

As mentioned above, the patient most likely has several therapists. It is the individual therapist's job to work at pulling all the therapists together. This does not necessarily mean regular and frequent meetings with all involved, in person. Instead, the therapist has to do the following:

1. Know about the existence of the other therapists. This is not always easy as the patient may consider the other therapists as "friends" she talks to. Eventually the patient will talk of some other professional who is giving them "help."
2. Contact all involved therapists for a meeting, ideally in person, about the patient. If this cannot be done in person by all, a telephone conversation should be set up when some time is available to discuss the patient.
3. During this communication, the therapist should take the initiative that the following are accomplished:

    a. Each therapist should know of the existence of the others, how they were engaged by the patient, and in what capacity they are functioning with the patient.
    b. Agreement should be reached as to who is the primary therapist to whom any pertinent information about the patient will be forwarded.
    c. Agreement should be reached about the diagnosis for the patient. Sometimes this is not possible because the patient has set up an effective splitting already. In such cases, the primary therapist should not argue vehemently but should comment on

the difference among the therapists about the diagnosis, perhaps because of the disparate presentations of the patient.

d. Explicit prediction should be made that the patient will set up differences among the therapists, and it should be acknowledged that these differences, when brought together, represent the total patient.

e. All should be aware of any patient-induced emotional resonance and perverse relating. Furthermore, all should be aware that the patient will be setting up situations where the therapists will inadvertently hold her back from functioning well. The patient will be attempting to function in an area where, based on her pathology, this seems impossible. If the therapists take a stance against it, the patient will have the reinforcement of feeling held back in a regressed position. It must be remembered that the patient is not simply splitting their own feelings about the task and provoking the therapist to take the negative side. Often patients may feel ambivalent about something they are about to do. They like it and want it, but also feel it may be impossible or dangerous. They may talk to the therapist in such a way that the therapist becomes very aware of the negative aspects of the endeavor and voices these negative aspects. At that moment, the patient is relieved of the ambivalence. She now keeps only the good aspects and argues with the therapist who is keeping the negative side for her. In the case of the BPD patient, it is not only the ambivalence that is handled this way, but it is also a replay of the patient's perception that the parental figure demands only regression on her part and will punish autonomy and well-being by emotional disconnection. All the therapists should be aware that allowing the patient to take growth steps will probably be frightening to themselves and to the patient.

f. Agreement should be reached that the patient will be told that all the therapists will occasionally communicate with one another for her benefit. This will facilitate the mending of the split at least on the intellectual level for the patient.

g. Agreement should be reached as to whether further communication among the therapists will be at regular intervals or under certain circumstances only.

As therapy progresses with all involved, usually the number of therapists drops. This is effected by the patient or the therapists themselves. This even reflects the better integration of the patient. While it may not mean that the patient no longer uses perverse relating, it does mean that the patient has developed trust that the main therapist is the most effective in relieving them of their intolerable affects and is the best at playing the corresponding part in this perverse relating. In other words, the patient may not be getting better but has found the best substitute for the original parental figure. The benefit is that a true one-to-one relationship has been established.

However, if the therapist has been a good container for the patient's feelings (i.e., a good digester of the patient-induced emotional resonance) and has been slowly trying to reverse the perverse relating, the patient has now chosen to be with the therapist who has given them a glimpse of the way out of their suffering. The patient has experienced mergers even after doing well. There has been no rejection or abandonment and no pushing toward regression. The mergers when doing poorly have been short and accompanied by clear messages by the therapist that this is not desired by the therapist and is bad for the patient. The overwhelming affects have been digested into more tolerable ones. At the same time, there has been no stimulation of these affects from threats of abandonment or threats of keeping the patient in the regressed and merged states. Now the patient can stay individuated for longer periods of time and can have remergers without creating pain for herself. The patient can continue the separation-individuation task.

Family Therapy

The patient with BPD will have family members around who are engaged in the same perverse relating with them as other people are. Frequently, these family members will call the therapist in panic, great fear, and urgency about the patient. Usually they are afraid that the patient is about to harm herself, and they feel they are impotent in stopping it. In other words, they feel the same as the therapist feels about the patient (i.e., they have accepted the emotional merging call of the patient on the basis of the patient's pain). The family usually wants the therapist not to tell the patient that they have called, for they are afraid that the patient will get very angry (i.e., they have previously experienced the patient's accusations and rage for the help, or merger, they have given).

I have found it helpful not to think of the family members as culprits who have started the whole situation. This is usually what the patient wants us to do and results in stories of tremendous emotional or physical abuse. Instead, I find it more helpful to remember that the patient has not been able to integrate the image of the bad parent with the image of the good parent, and thus the bad-parent image is felt as overwhelmingly bad. I remember that this overwhelmingly bad parent has also been described to me by the same patient as quite good. It is often hard to reconstruct how the whole perverse relating began with the patient and the mother. Was the mother caught in this kind of relating because of the patient's strong pull for this even in infancy, like the therapist is in the beginning of therapy and as other people in the patient's life are? Was she so exhausted with the child's pulling for mergers in crisis that when the child was independent, she was afraid to receive the child in a warm union? Or, did the mother herself push for this kind of relating because of her own difficulties? Ultimately, however, this question is not that relevant here and now as we help the patient.

Rather, the relevant questions are, "Who in the patient's life is now caught in the perverse relating? Who needs help in surviving this relating without rejecting and emotionally or physically abandoning the patient? Who can be helped to change for their sake and the patient's sake?" Because of these questions, I always involve, in the beginning, the family members who interact with the patient.

I find proceeding in the following way helps:

1. After I arrive at the diagnosis of BPD, I make sure that I find out about the present family interactions with the patient in as much detail as possible. Usually that is not so difficult as the patient will often complain that the family is not managing their "depression" well.
2. I then tell the patient that I would like to talk with the family members who are involved in order to help their situation at home. If the family has already called, I have an opening for this suggestion to the patient. Usually the patient accepts the suggestion willingly, wanting the therapist to stop the family from "taking their freedom away."
3. If the family has called, I tell them that I understand their fear and frustration and that I shall work with the patient on the problem they have told me, but I must tell the patient about their call. I point out that it is not possible for me to work on the problem they told me about without telling the patient how I found out about the situation. If I do not disclose the source of my information, the

patient will either think I am clairvoyant or will know the family has told me. Since the patient is usually based in reality enough to know I could not be clairvoyant, she will definitely know the information is coming from the family behind her back, which only supplies more reasons to feel angry at the family. I tell the family that while I understand their fear of the patient's rage very well—and that I share their fear that she will hurt herself—we must tell the patient of our communication. I emphasize that telling the patient about our communication is the only chance for me and us to be of help to the patient. I recommend that the family tells the patient about the call because they were concerned for her, but if they cannot do that, I shall tell the patient of their call and concern. This interaction becomes my first therapeutic interventions with the family because of the following:

a. They experience the digestion of their own feelings via my sharing and toleration of these feelings. It must be remembered that the patient has set up the emotional resonance with them, just as they do with the therapist. The family is showing these feelings to us and, in effect, recreating the emotional resonance with us.
b. I give suggestions to the family for telling the patient of the call. I might say, "Tell her, 'I called Dr. Albanese because I was worried about you when you said you are going to buy a gun. You may be angry about this, but I do think you gave a message of also wanting help.'" The family now has the knowledge that I will give them concrete help in how to talk to the patient. They have a way out of the sense of paralysis they feel when they want to talk to the patient when it can seem that no matter what they say, something catastrophic can happen.
c. This also establishes the anticipation that interactions with me, the therapist, will not lead into blaming them for the patient's problems.
d. In general, I try to convey to the family, in all my interactions with them, that I am knowledgeable, nonaccusatory, empathic, and trustworthy.

4. When I set up the meeting with the family for the first time, I give a choice to the patient of being there or not. I say that it is preferable that she is there during the meeting, but if is she does not wish to

do so, I shall do my best to relate to her everything that was said at the meeting. I say, nonetheless, that we should have some meetings together afterward. The reason I do not insist that the patient be there is that I am giving her choices and asking for her own input into her therapy. I am trying to minimize the feeling that I am taking over for her.
5. I do not give the same choice to the family. If the patient chooses not to be there at the first meeting, the family usually feels relieved. If, however, the patient does choose to be there for the first meeting, I assure the family that I will help them say the important things in front of the patient. I tell them that, this way, the patient will know they care for her, regardless of how angry she may get at the time. I also tell the family that I have arrived at some conclusions about the patient and that I shall tell them of these conclusions at the meeting. This gives them hope that something concretely helpful may happen and that they will not have the whole burden of "telling on" the patient and enduring the emotional attacks.

During the meeting with the family, I do the following:

1. After the greetings, I open up the meeting by saying something like "I am glad we are all here, for I know that all of us here are concerned for the well-being of . . . (I give the patient's name). I know that things have been difficult for all." If the patient is not there, I proceed to talk in the terms the family has given me as to what the difficulties are. I make sure that I talk, at first, more than the family.

    This is done in contrast to what I might do with the families of patients who do not have BPD problems. This, again, is to establish for the family a sense of safety and comfort that I shall not let them flounder as they have previously had to do with the patient.
2. After the initial opening by me, I ask the family to talk of their concerns and observations.

    During their recounting, I interpose empathic statements as to how they must have felt when the patient did . . . (something that was concerning to the family). I say something like, "Oh my!" or "That must have been so frightening!" or "One cannot know what to do in situations like that!" or "It is so frustrating!"

3. I make sure to find out what the family has done when the patient had shown them this concerning behavior. Their actions usually fall into one of the following three categories:

   a. Trying to be very supportive and directly helpful, such as by taking medicines away, giving money, exhorting not to do hurtful things, and so on.
   b. Since the patient's behavior always reappears and gets worse after their help, the family members may have exploded into rage. At times, some have shouted and even hit the patient.
   c. The family may have become exhausted and will pay no attention to the patient's emotional and hurtful behavior. Some will actually cut contact with the patient.

   Most family members will volunteer only the supportive actions they have taken toward the patient. I make sure to state to them that the patient's behavior also always evokes much frustration. I state that a person can come to the point of feeling "I can't take it anymore! I give up!"

   Whatever the family discloses, I respond in the same, nonjudgmental manner. I say that it is understandable why they did what they did, and I ask what the patient's response was to their intervention. Invariably, the response to what they tried to do was not good, and the patient has accused them of being controlling and invasive. I again state, "One cannot know what to do!"

4. At this point I ask the family whether there have been peaceful and happy interactions with the patient in the recent past, such as family get-togethers, going out to eat, going out shopping, playing games, and so on. Also was there anything they may have liked to do in the past? The answer is usually "no." It is impossible to have a happy time with the patient when she seems to always be in a crisis.

   Some relative, usually but not necessarily the mother, states that she can have no peace, worrying constantly about the patient.

5. Now I state that it is clear they care so much for their child. I explain that their child seems to have difficulty growing up and is hanging on to them with these emotional behaviors but then accuses them of not letting her grow. Irrespective of the family members' own difficulties, they always seem to understand and appreciate this statement. I then say that the patient was probably always a more

difficult child, maybe she was born more emotional. This usually brings out stories to confirm it. I point out that they and the patient have become caught in strong emotional tie only in crises. They have the emotional tie because they care for each other. However, they all hate the unhappiness that is always set up with this tie as evidenced by the patient's accusations and the family's feelings of frustration They all long for a happy sense of being together.

If the patient is present, I slightly alter my statements to also include the patient's point of view. I state that it is clear they care for each other and that this is why the family tries to help. I state that the patient knows this and seeks their help one way or another (here I give any previously recounted examples). I make sure to address the patient saying, "You probably always wanted to feel strong on your own and to feel independent."

6. If the patient is actively in emotional crisis during the meeting with the family, I pay attention to the emotional resonance set up with me. I say exactly the same things to the patient as if we were alone. I only add, while addressing the family, "This is also like how you must feel: wanting to help and not knowing how," and "We all (I wave my hand to indicate all present) sometimes just feel afraid and frustrated." I do this to help the patient with the overwhelming feeling at the time, to help the family with their own feeling set up by the patient, and to teach the family by example.

7. I state that we all have to learn to be together in positive, strong emotions and not only with the painful situations. I say this will be difficult and frightening. I then explain the therapeutic parameters between the patient and myself.

8. At this point, I may not offer family sessions, for I wish to see what the effect of this meeting will have. I do tell the family that what the patient and I discuss is confidential, but that if they feel very worried and call, I will take it up with the patient so that something can be done.

Most of the time, the family does not call too frequently. If they do, I then set up a defined number of family sessions. This is never more than ten. The intervals are not the same, and I space out the sessions at my judgment, with varying time in-between sessions, depending on crises. The sessions are usually a month apart, but they may be a week to six months apart. I make sure not to give the message of tremendous fear to the family.

9. At the end of the session, I give a suggestion to the family to do something together that is fun and happy. I have them decide, together with the patient, what the activity shall be. I forewarn them that it will be hard at first not to talk about the difficulties or get upset. But they must endeavor to drop any discussions of difficulties. I say to the patient that it may seem to her the family does not care if she feels very unhappy during the activity. If things do not work out at first, eventually they will, I assure them. I also point out that as a family, they had shown much strength and, no matter what, they will be together. This I say to the entire group, or I address it to the duo that is most involved, such as the mother and patient. This is done not to threaten that I shall separate them; if they feel secure in not losing the other, they can venture more confidently into emotional separation.
10. If I have to call for family sessions, during the session there is a repetition of the first meeting, with emphasis on recent crisis. Almost invariably it is precipitated by the patient's fear of perceived abandonment, which can be caused by her own steps toward independence, praise by the family, or, sometimes, the involved family member has been busy with their own life and has not been available to the patient. The work in the sessions is always to pay attention to the emotional resonance, to remind all that crises have been survived before, and to reinforce the positive aspects of relating.

At times, it becomes clear that another family member has serious emotional problem which necessitates referral for therapy somewhere else. This usually evokes mixed feelings in the patient, who feels relieved that her perceptions are confirmed but also feels frightened that this now leads to abandonment or guilt that she caused the problems, if the patient is capable of feeling guilt.

If it becomes clear that the patient was seriously abused by a family member in the past, separation from this member has to occur. This may be difficult while the patient is involved in perverse relating with the family member, thus sticking with the one who has hurt her. In my experience, I have not found many cases of such abuse in BPD patients who demonstrate the above-described relating pathology. I have seen it, however, in patients who may fit the *DSM-IV-TR* criteria for the diagnosis and may involve themselves in hurtful relationships. They also show splitting of how they perceive the hurtful person. When this person is hurtful, they complain and say they will leave the situation, but when this person is nice to them, they totally forget this and feel all is well. However, these patients do not present to the therapists demanding the perverse relationship with them, and they do not get worse at any attempt to help them. Furthermore, they depend on empathy rather than emotional resonance to feel better. When we are with them, we feel very sorry and outraged for them and are motivated to help. But we do not have feelings without being aware that the patient feels the same. In the case when the patient uses emotional resonance, we often are not aware that the patient has similar feelings as we do and is evoking them in us. We feel that the feelings are only ours. Additionally, these patients will respond to praise positively. In other words, they have negotiated the individuation more successfully.

Group Therapy

I find group therapy helpful to reinforce nonperverse relating. It is also good to help patients identify the precipitating factors before an emotional crisis and self-hurting behavior or rage occurs. However, a group does not easily behave as a successful resonator for the emotions set up by the patient in the group members. Often the group becomes overly upset and frightened, with the patient then escalating the emotional turmoil. The therapist has the job of not only serving as a digester for the feelings of the patient but must also do the same for the entire group. This can become too overwhelming to the therapist. The other patients themselves may have their own problems exaggerated by the emotionality set up by the patient. Conversely, the group members may get exhausted by the patient and totally turn off from responding to the BPD patient's plea for a response. They can also get angry at the therapist for continuing to "be manipulated by the patient" (as they can begin to believe) and for not giving them the attention they need. If the group therapist abruptly drops the attention they have been giving to the patient, the patient can attempt suicide, resulting in devastating guilt in other patients and the therapist.

Group therapy with these patients is wrought with difficulties. I think it is best done only after the crises have subsided for the patient. Furthermore, it cannot provide the one-to-one separation-individuation needed by the patient. I think it can be helpful, however, if the patient has another individual therapist, the frequent crises are over, and the group therapy is conducted by two therapists. The two therapists can help to prevent one another from being overwhelmed and thus keep their responses less emotionally driven, while continuing to provide balance for the other patients. It is also imperative that the group therapists and the individual therapist keep in touch for the reasons described above. I have been in the position of being a group therapist or an individual therapist for BPD patients and found that when the above criteria are met, things can work out. Another caveat is that the individual therapist and the group therapist should never be the same person. This principle is good to observe no matter what the patient's diagnosis is.

Chapter 6

Medication

In describing the above therapeutic approach, I must have given the impression that medication has no place in the treatment of the BPD patient.

While I have seen both effective treatment without medication and helpful contribution by the medication, in this book I have chosen to concentrate mainly on the therapeutic technique as a thorough discussion about medication is beyond the scope of this book.

Nonetheless, medication can diminish the intensity of affect in these patients, making the therapeutic work a little easier. When medication is used, it is important to keep in mind the following:

1. The act of prescribing medication usually conveys to the patient that someone else, the prescribing doctor and the medication, will take over. This represents merger with the concomitant "stifling" effect on the patient. It is thus important to always involve the patient about the decision to use medication and even to choose which medication that may be. The doctor must take the active part of factually educating about the available medication. The doctor must always predict that the medication will not take all the pain away and that it will very likely cause unpleasant side effects. I usually end a discussion like that with "I don't know. We could try. It may help a little. What do you think?"
2. The patient is likely to escalate their need for medication. The medication seems to help for a short while, and then the patient gets worse. The doctor then increases the dose and adds new medication.

In spite of the side effects this is continued and escalated since the patient seems to be in dire danger and need of intervention via medication. Thus a down-spiraling cycle can be enacted with the medication. If the doctor is aware of this cycle, the addition of more medication can be avoided. If I see that the patient is escalating requests or needs for medication, yet has severe side effects, I say to myself that I am actually in the perverse relating set up by the patient. I give medication to help, and I end up hurting the patient. I feel guilty if I do not try to help and guilty when I do try to help. I feel incompetent, afraid, frustrated, angry, and trapped. This is how the patient must feel. The emotional resonance is also set up. Thus I take the opposite action and say, "I see that the medication did not help. You have side effects and feel the same, if not worse. I think that we must actually diminish the medication. I am not helping with it, and I seem to be just making you feel worse."

3. The patient may use the medication to try suicide or to inflict pain on herself. Medication can become just another means of hurting herself. One must be aware of the potentiality of the patient using medication for this purpose and be aware of which medication can be more easily lethal—such as Lithium, MAO inhibitors, tricyclics, and so on. Benzodiazepines may diminish the anxiety but do not diminish the tension these patients have and can actually allow for greater anger expression, not to mention their addictive potential. I have been surprised, however, on several occasions, that a BPD patient, seemingly addicted to benzodiazepines, was able to drop the "addiction" relatively easily. This change would occur when their addiction no longer served to bind them to anyone and another mode of hurting themselves took over in eliciting binding behavior with a person.

4. Medication gives the message to the patient that, intrinsically, they are not able to "do on their own." It gives a regressive and "lack of confidence" message to the patient. It works best if it is used with the anticipation by the doctor and the patient that it is only a temporary measure. This gives the patient confidence that they can exist on their own.

I have used the terms "doctor" and "therapist" interchangeably. Splitting the tasks of medication prescription and therapy between two people is especially wrought with difficulty. The one who gives therapy, when pushed to great fear by the patient, can delegate the emotion-taming of the patient to the medication prescriber. Thus, there is no full containment of the affect for the patient via emotional resonance and, thus, lack of growth. The medication prescriber, on the other hand, is usually not aware of the life-precipitating events to the emotional crises and inadvertently promotes the patient's relinquishing of self-control. Or the prescribing doctor, especially if time is restricted, can inadvertently get caught in the ever-escalating cycles described above. There is also always great potential for splitting the two therapists, which the patient unconsciously creates. The therapists can feel annoyed with one another as each feels the other is mismanaging the patient.

Because of the above difficulties, I recommend that the same therapist does therapy and prescribes medication, if need be. Alternatively, I recommend that the patient be in therapy without medication. If division of the tasks of therapy and medication is inevitable, communication between the two must be very effective, and both must have the same understanding of the dynamics of the patient. The goal in such cases must be the eventual reduction or removal of the medication and the dependency on the prescribing doctor.

I say that the goal must be stopping of the medication in the future; this may not be possible for some patients. Some may have a very strong, biological, emotional intensity, which the medication can tame. However, the medication must always be instituted with the specifically stated goal that it shall be time-limited. This is, as described above, in order to give the message that

1. I do not intend to bind you with me at the expense of your competence and strength; and
2. It is in you, the wish and the ability, to grow and be strong.

The patient must be given total freedom for full growth. When the perverse relating subsides—the emotional resonance is no longer primarily used for tolerance of emotion, and the patient has developed other mechanisms of defense—medication can usually be slowly stopped. Depending on the strength of the constitutional predisposition for great intensity of affect, the patient may or may not do well enough without medication. Some may become overwhelmed with affect again and revert to old means of handling it. Others may have great intensity of affect, but they have achieved enough individuation and have picked up enough other mechanisms of defense (other than emotional resonance and splitting) that they do not revert back. When the latter type of patient does need medication, they react to it as other patients without BPD do: they do not show the complications described above.

Summary and Conclusions

As I summarize, I wish to emphasize that my comments are about treatment for the patient with a BPD diagnosis, who also demonstrates a particular interpersonal relating I call "perverse relating." This is the patient who asks for help while in an obviously desperate state and then, when given the help, reacts negatively, usually conveying the message that the help was "stifling." The same patient does not leave the therapist because they have been bad to them but comes back. The patient is never experienced as an "easy patient," and the therapist often dreads working with them and wishes to get rid of them but may feel bound to stay because "it is too dangerous to let them go."

I hope to have dispelled some of the thoughts that these patients are hopeless and that we are unable to help. Knowledge of some basic dynamics about these patients can provide us with the guidance to help them and the optimism that they can be helped.

My way of dealing with the patient is only one way of doing so. Dialectical behavioral therapy, transference-focused therapy, relationship management therapy, and mentalization-based therapy, and some other supportive therapies, using other words and actions, also work with the patient's psychodynamic state. The reader can develop his or her own style, using the psychodynamic principles described.

What follows is a summary of the information I've discussed in this book:

1. The patient is truly in an emotionally overwhelming crisis and is undergoing behavioral discontrol, on and off. This is in no way manipulative to get something. These patients truly get overwhelmed by emotion. This may be because there is a biological predisposition to feel more strongly than others or because they have not been given

the opportunity to modulate the feelings as others have them or a combination of both. It is essential to accept this fact that they are overwhelmed when working with these patients.

2. The therapist's emotional turmoil, and sometimes their behavior, can seem overreactive; rather, it is a response to the patient's pressure on the therapist. These patients, more than most, are excellent in affecting the therapist's feelings and actions. The mistakes made with them are, more often than not, a clue to the patient's emotional need from us. When they communicate with us, verbally or otherwise, it is for two main reasons: one is to tell us how bad they feel, and the second is to make us feel the same. When the therapist feels very strongly about the BPD patient—even if negatively so—it is a sign that this therapist has taken the first steps toward being therapeutic with this patient.

3. When they make us feel a strong, negative feeling, such as fear and anger, it is not because they are angry at us or wish to hurt us sadistically. It is because they feel those feelings themselves. It is not helpful to say "You made me angry." Instead, it is helpful to say "I feel angry," without attributing the blame for this feeling to the patient. However, we must be aware that the patient has said and done things for the purpose of evoking our feelings so that we can "share it with them."

4. The patients have good antennas as to how we experience the feelings they have evoked in us. They will automatically emotionally follow our own emotional state, as if they are now "sharing with us" their feelings. They lower the intensity of their overwhelming feelings through the "sharing." This has been called "projective identification" and I call it "patient-induced emotional resonance." The therapist has a true tool in helping the patient by paying attention to this mechanism. There are a variety of ways that the therapist can show acceptance of the feelings from the patient and return a more palatable version of this feeling to the patient.

5. Abandonment is the injury that evokes the overwhelming feelings in the patients. They seek to abolish their individuation in order not to feel the abandonment. They achieve abolition of individuation by pain to themselves and through the emotional sameness they evoke in us. This sameness helps them diminish the feelings, but when that occurs, they switch to no longer being able to tolerate the loss of individuation to us. Then, they complain that we are stifling

and controlling them. Thus, one should always remember to involve the patient in decisions yet never to let the patient make decisions without some input by the therapist. We must "sit on the border" with them.

6. The BPD patient desperately wishes to stop having to heal the overwhelming abandonment feelings by causing pain to themselves. However, they have no experience of having such feelings healed in any other way, and they expect abandonment when they do well. The therapist must be sensitive to this dilemma and not push the patient into wellness. The therapist's job is to convince the patient that there shall be no emotional abandonment when the patient is strong and well. This can be done by saying to the patient, "I want you to be strong and happy. I do not want you to have pain." It can be demonstrated by judicious availability and confidence that the patient is able to take up tasks that seem impossible to them.

7. Do not be discouraged by setbacks. These must occur. It is important to have patience in the long run; no one grows with only one good meal.

8. These patients need help in identifying precipitants to the emotional turmoil. Do not fall for the "broken mind-brain theory" as I call the explanation of the symptoms of these patients. Even though they may have a biological predisposition to exaggerated emotional responses, there is always an interpersonal event that has worked as a precipitant to their symptoms.

9. Likewise, these patients need to feel, identify, and name feelings other than overwhelming separation affect and rage. At first, the therapist must do that for them.

10. Use the splitting that has been set up by the patient to become aware of all aspects of the patient.

11. The therapist's work with these patients is taxing. The therapist should always have someone to whom he or she can turn to establish emotional equanimity and pull back to rational decisions when overwhelmed.

12. With or without direct exhortation to more adaptive behavior, these patients will surprise you by eventually coming with more adaptive and "run of the mill" behaviors. They will have calmer affective experiences of traumas that, in the past, had overwhelmed them. They will show a wider repertoire of affective states that they

themselves will name. Ultimately, you will no longer have to feel their feelings but only have empathy for them.

The BPD person is going around giving the message "Please help me. I need to feel assured that I shall not be abandoned if I am well. I need to feel assured that you do not demand of me pain so that you do not abandon me. I do not like losing my individuation, and I do not like to be in pain. I need to know there is something else for me. For now, I need you to be with me just as I am and for you to share all of my pain. Eventually, I will learn that you can share my strengths also. Then I will feel sane and be like others."

As a therapist, know that you can actually come to look forward to having the BPD patient come to see you—they will become no longer a dread, but a joy in the office.

Bibliography

Kernberg, O. F. (1975). *Borderline Conditions and Pathological Narcissism.* Lanham, MD: Jason Aronson.

Mahler, M. S. (1968). *On Human Symbiosis and the Vicissitudes of Individuation.* New York: International Universities Press.

Masterson, J. F. (1976). *Psychotherapy of the Borderline Adult.* Bristol, PA: Brunner/Mazel.

Ogden, T. H. (1982). *Projective Identification and Psychotherapeutic Technique.* Lanham, MD: Jason Aronson.